List of
Species

W0007622

Complimentary with

The Fragile Forest
inside Brazilian **Amazonia**

Published by
International Fine Art Gallery
Augusta, USA

Partial list of Amazon diversity
Mammals, Birds, Reptiles, Fish, Amphibians

Front Cover:
Top (L-R): Silky Anteater, Colourful Ornamental Fish
Bottom (L-R): The Green Iguana, Silver Beaked Tanager

Back Cover:
Brazil Nut Pod (photo: Miguel Moran)

List compiled in cooperation with
International Union for Conservation of Nature (IUCN)

Design & Printing:
www.parishree.com

Published by:
International Fine Art Gallery
406, 8th Street, Augusta, GA 30901, USA
Tel: +1 706 826 1897
Fax: +1 706 826 4827
Email: valledolmo@att.net

All rights reserved. No part of this book
may be reproduced, in any form or by any
means, electronic or mechanical, including
photocopying, recording or by any information
storage and retrieval system, without
permission in writing from the publisher.

First Print: 2010

Printed in India

The Amazon rainforest, despite its threatened status, remains the largest continuous tropical forest in the world. It contains a fifth of all the known plants on earth: Scientists have identified an astounding 90,000 living plants in a single square kilometre of the Amazon rainforest, and more than 75,000 types of tree in the vast basin.

In such a rich and complex biodiversity region, an exhaustive compilation of other living beings is by no means an easy task. While the number of species of native mammals is still being researched and identified, the bulk of its fauna comprises insect species, which are difficult to enumerate even roughly.

Readers of this book are informed that this is only a partial list of mammals, birds, reptiles, amphibians and fish complied to accompany the book The Fragile Forest: Inside Brazilian Amazonia. The list is compiled in cooperation with the International Union for Conservation of Nature (IUCN), and several other experts and is by no means a detailed and comprehensive list.

Family	Species	Common names (Eng)
Cricetidae	*Ruschii*	Rushi's Rat
Cricetidae	*Azarae*	Azara's Grass Mouse
Cricetidae	*Cursor*	Cursor Grass Mouse, Cusorial Akodont
Cricetidae	*Lindberghi*	Lindbergh's Grass Mouse
Cricetidae	*Montensis*	Montane Akodont
Cricetidae	*Paranaensis*	Paraná Akodont
Cricetidae	*Sanctipaulensis*	Sao Paulo Grass Mouse
Cricetidae	*Serrensis*	Serrado Do Mar Grass Mouse
Atelidae	*Belzebul*	Red-handed Howler Monkey
Atelidae	*Caraya*	Black-and-gold Howler Monkey
Atelidae	*Discolor*	Spix's Red-handed Howler Monkey
Atelidae	*Guariba*	Brown Howler Monkey
Atelidae	*Juara*	Juruá Red Howler Monkey
Atelidae	*Macconnelli*	Guianan Red Howler Monkey
Atelidae	*Nigerrima*	Black Howler Monkey
Atelidae	*Puruensis*	Purús Red Howler Monkey
Atelidae	*Seniculus*	Colombian Red Howler Monkey
Atelidae	*Ululata*	Maranhão Red-handed Howler Monkey
Phyllostomidae	*Centurio*	Little White-shouldered Bat
Phyllostomidae	*Caudifer*	Tailed Tailless Bat
Phyllostomidae	*Geoffroyi*	Geoffroy's Tailless Bat
Aotidae	*Nigriceps*	Black-headed Night Monkey
Aotidae	*Trivirgatus*	Night Monkey
Otariidae	*Australis*	South American Fur Seal
Phyllostomidae	*Anderseni*	Andersen's Fruit-eating Bat
Phyllostomidae	*Cinereus*	Gervais's Fruit-eating Bat
Phyllostomidae	*Concolor*	Brown Fruit-eating Bat
Phyllostomidae	*Fimbriatus*	Fringed Fruit-eating Bat
Phyllostomidae	*Glaucus*	Silver Fruit-eating Bat
Phyllostomidae	*Gnomus*	Dwarf Fruit-eating Bat
Phyllostomidae	*Lituratus*	Great Fruit-eating Bat
Phyllostomidae	*Obscurus*	Dark Fruit-eating Bat
Phyllostomidae	*Phaeotis*	Pygmy Fruit-eating Bat
Phyllostomidae	*Planirostris*	Flat-faced Fruit-eating Bat
Atelidae	*Belzebuth*	Long-haired Spider Monkey
Atelidae	*Chamek*	Black-faced Black Spider Monkey
Atelidae	*Marginatus*	White-cheeked Spider Monkey
Atelidae	*Paniscus*	Guiana Spider Monkey
Balaenopteridae	*Acutorostrata*	Common Minke Whale
Balaenopteridae	*Bonaerensis*	Antarctic Minke Whale

Family	Species	Common names (Eng)
Balaenopteridae	Borealis	Sei Whale
Balaenopteridae	Edeni	Bryde's Whale
Balaenopteridae	Musculus	Blue Whale
Balaenopteridae	Physalus	Fin Whale
Procyonidae	Beddardi	Beddard's Olingo
Ziphiidae	Arnuxii	Southern Four-toothed Whale
Cricetidae	Labiosus	Large-lipped Crimson-nosed Rat
Cricetidae	Breviceps	Brazilian Shrew Mouse
Cervidae	Dichotomus	Marsh Deer
Atelidae	Arachnoides	Woolly Spider Monkey
Atelidae	Hypoxanthus	Northern Muriqui
Bradypodidae	Torquatus	Maned Three-toed Sloth
Bradypodidae	Tridactylus	Pale-throated Three-toed Sloth
Cricetidae	Iheringi	Ihering's Hocicudo
Dasypodidae	Tatouay	Greater Naked-tailed Armadillo
Dasypodidae	Unicinctus	Southern Naked-tailed Armadillo
Pitheciidae	Ayresi	Ayres Black Uakari
Pitheciidae	Calvus	Bald-headed Uacari
Pitheciidae	Hosomi	Black-headed Uacari
Pitheciidae	Melanocephalus	Golden-backed Black Uakari
Callitrichidae	Humilis	Black-crowned Dwarf Marmoset
Pitheciidae	Baptista	Baptista Lake Titi Monkey
Pitheciidae	Brunneus	Brown Titi Monkey
Pitheciidae	Caligatus	Chestnut-bellied Titi
Pitheciidae	Cinerascens	Ashy Black Titi Monkey
Pitheciidae	Cupreus	Coppery Titi Monkey
Pitheciidae	Lucifer	Yellow-handed Titi Monkey
Pitheciidae	Lugens	Collared Titi
Pitheciidae	Melanochir	Coastal Black-handed Titi
Pitheciidae	Moloch	Red-bellied Titi Monkey
Pitheciidae	Nigrifrons	Black-fronted Titi Monkey
Pitheciidae	Personatus	Atlantic Titi
Pitheciidae	Torquatus	Collared Titi Monkey
Echimyidae	Pictus	Painted Tree-rat
Callitrichidae	Aurita	Buffy-tufted-ear Marmoset
Callitrichidae	Flaviceps	Buffy-headed Marmoset
Callitrichidae	Geoffroyi	White-fronted Marmoset
Callitrichidae	Jacchus	Common Marmoset
Callitrichidae	Kuhlii	Wied's Black-tufted-ear Marmoset
Callitrichidae	Penicillata	Black-pencilled Marmoset

Family	Species	Common names (Eng)
Cricetidae	*Callosus*	Large Vesper Mouse
Cricetidae	*Hummelincki*	Hummelinck's Vesper Mouse
Cricetidae	*Laucha*	Small Vesper Mouse
Cricetidae	*Tener*	Delicate Vesper Mouse
Didelphidae	*Lanatus*	Brown-eared Wooly Opossum
Didelphidae	*Philander*	Bare-tailed Woolly Opossum
Didelphidae	*Irrupta*	Black-shouldered Opossum
Phyllostomidae	*Brevicauda*	Silky Short-tailed Bat
Phyllostomidae	*Castanea*	Chestnut Short-tailed Bat
Phyllostomidae	*Perspicillata*	Seba's Short-tailed Bat
Echimyidae	*Sulcidens*	Owl's Spiny Rat
Caviidae	*Aperea*	Brazilian Guinea Pig
Caviidae	*Fulgida*	Shiny Guinea Pig
Caviidae	*Magna*	Greater Guinea Pig
Callitrichidae	*Pygmaea*	Pygmy Marmoset
Cebidae	*Albifrons*	White-fronted Capuchin
Cebidae	*Apella*	Black-capped Capuchin
Cebidae	*Cay*	Hooded Capuchin
Cebidae	*Flavius*	Blonde Capuchin
Cebidae	*Libidinosus*	Bearded Capuchin
Cebidae	*Macrocephalus*	Large-headed Capuchin
Cebidae	*Nigritus*	Black-horned Capuchin
Cebidae	*Olivaceus*	Weeper Capuchin
Cebidae	*Robustus*	Crested Capuchin
Cebidae	*Xanthosternos*	Yellow-breasted Capuchin
Emballonuridae	*Maximiliani*	Shaggy Bat
Canidae	*Thous*	Crab-eating Fox
Cricetidae	*Subflavus*	Terraced Rice Rat
Erethizontidae	*Subspinosus*	Bristle-spined Rat
Phyllostomidae	*Doriae*	Brazilian Big-eyed Bat
Phyllostomidae	*Trinitatum*	Little Big-eyed Bat
Phyllostomidae	*Villosum*	Hairy Big-eyed Bat
Didelphidae	*Minimus*	Water Opossum
Pitheciidae	*Albinasus*	Red-nosed Bearded Saki
Pitheciidae	*Chiropotes*	Bearded Saki
Pitheciidae	*Satanas*	Black Bearded Saki
Phyllostomidae	*Minor*	Lesser Long-tailed Bat
Megalonychidae	*Didactylus*	Linné'S Two-toed Sloth
Megalonychidae	*Hoffmanni*	Hoffmann's Two-toed Sloth
Phyllostomidae	*Auritus*	Big-eared Wooly Bat

Family	Species	Common names (Eng)
Canidae	*Brachyurus*	Maned Wolf
Erethizontidae	*Nycthemera*	Koopman's Porcupine
Erethizontidae	*Prehensilis*	Brazilian Porcupine
Mephitidae	*Chinga*	Molina's Hog-nosed Skunk
Mephitidae	*Semistriatus*	Amazonian Hog-nosed Skunk
Emballonuridae	*Brevirostris*	Chestnut Sac-winged Bat
Didelphidae	*Agricolai*	Agricola's Gracile Opossum
Ctenomyidae	*Brasiliensis*	Brazilian Tuco-tuco
Ctenomyidae	*Flamarioni*	Tuco-tuco Of The Dunes
Ctenomyidae	*Minutus*	Tiny Tuco-tuco
Ctenomyidae	*Torquatus*	Collared Tuco-tuco
Cuniculidae	*Paca*	Spotted Paca
Cyclopedidae	*Didactylus*	Silky Anteater
Molossidae	*Paranus*	Brown Dog-faced Bat
Molossidae	*Planirostris*	Southern Dog-faced Bat
Emballonuridae	*Alecto*	Short-eared Bat
Echimyidae	*Boliviensis*	Bolivian Bamboo Rat
Echimyidae	*Dactylinus*	Amazon Bamboo Rat
Dasyproctidae	*Azarae*	Azara's Agouti
Dasyproctidae	*Fuliginosa*	Black Agouti
Dasyproctidae	*Leporina*	Red-rumped Agouti
Dasyproctidae	*Prymnolopha*	Black-rumped Agouti
Dasyproctidae	*Punctata*	Central American Agouti
Dasypodidae	*Hybridus*	Southern Long-nosed Armadillo
Dasypodidae	*Kappleri*	Greater Long-nosed Armadillo
Dasypodidae	*Novemcinctus*	Common Long-nosed Armadillo
Dasypodidae	*Septemcinctus*	Brazilian Lesser Long-nosed Armadillo
Cricetidae	*Collinus*	Montane Delomys
Cricetidae	*Dorsalis*	Striped Atlantic Forest Rat
Cricetidae	*Sublineatus*	Pallid Atlantic Forest Rat
Cricetidae	*Kempi*	Kemp's Grass Mouse
Phyllostomidae	*Draculae*	Giant Vampire Bat
Phyllostomidae	*Youngi*	White-winged Vampire Bat
Emballonuridae	*Albus*	Northern Ghost Bat
Emballonuridae	*Ingens*	Greater Ghost Bat
Emballonuridae	*Isabellus*	Isabelle's Ghost Bat
Emballonuridae	*Scutatus*	Lesser Ghost Bat
Didelphidae	*Albiventris*	White-eared Opossum
Didelphidae	*Aurita*	Big-eared Opossum
Dinomyidae	*Branickii*	Pacarana

Family	Species	Common names (Eng)
Phyllostomidae	*Ecaudata*	Hairy-legged Vampire Bat
Echimyidae	*Chrysurus*	White-faced Tree Rat
Mustelidae	*Barbara*	Greyheaded Tayra
Vespertilionidae	*Brasiliensis*	Brazilian Brown Bat
Vespertilionidae	*Diminutus*	Diminutive Serotine
Vespertilionidae	*Fuscus*	Big Brown Bat
Balaenidae	*Australis*	Southern Right Whale
Molossidae	*Auripendulus*	Black Bonneted Bat
Molossidae	*Bonariensis*	Dwarf Bonneted Bat
Molossidae	*Dabbenei*	Big Bonneted Bat
Molossidae	*Glaucinus*	Wagner's Bonneted Bat
Molossidae	*Hansae*	Sanborn's Bonneted Bat
Molossidae	*Perotis*	Greater Bonneted Bat
Dasypodidae	*Sexcinctus*	Six-banded Armadillo
Cricetidae	*Emmonsae*	Emmons's Rice Rat
Cricetidae	*Lamia*	Monster Rice Rat
Cricetidae	*Macconnelli*	Macconnell's Rice Rat
Cricetidae	*Nitidus*	Elegant Rice Rat
Cricetidae	*Russatus*	Russet Rice Rat
Echimyidae	*Spinosus*	Guiara
Delphinidae	*Attenuata*	Slender Blackfish
Furipteridae	*Horrens*	Thumbless Bat
Caviidae	*Flavidens*	Yellow-toothed Cavy
Caviidae	*Spixii*	Spix's Yellow-toothed Cavy
Mustelidae	*Cuja*	Lesser Grison
Mustelidae	*Vittata*	Greater Grison
Didelphidae	*Venusta*	Bushy-tailed Opossum
Delphinidae	*Melas*	Long-finned Pilot Whale
Phyllostomidae	*Commissarisi*	Commissaris's Long-tongued Bat
Phyllostomidae	*Longirostris*	Miller's Long-tongued Bat
Phyllostomidae	*Soricina*	Pallas's Long-tongued Bat
Phyllostomidae	*Behnii*	Behni's Big-eared Bat, Behn's Bat
Phyllostomidae	*Daviesi*	Davies's Big-eared Bat
Phyllostomidae	*Sylvestris*	Tricolored Bat
Didelphidae	*Agilis*	Agile Gracile Mouse Opossum
Delphinidae	*Griseus*	Risso's Dolphin
Cricetidae	*Griseoflavus*	Gray Leaf-eared Mouse
Vespertilionidae	*Alienus*	Strange Big-eared Brown Bat
Vespertilionidae	*Montanus*	Small Big-eared Brown Bat
Vespertilionidae	*Velatus*	Tropical Big-eared Brown Bat

Family	Species	Common names (Eng)
Cricetidae	*Brasiliensis*	Web-footed Marsh Rat
Cricetidae	*Sciureus*	Marsh Rat
Hominidae	*Sapiens*	Human
Caviidae	*Hydrochaeris*	Capybara
Didelphidae	*Kalinowskii*	Kalinowski's Mouse Opossum
Cricetidae	*Laticeps*	Large-headed Rice Rat
Cricetidae	*Oniscus*	Sowbug Rice Rat
Cricetidae	*Yunganus*	Yungas Rice Rat
Ziphiidae	*Planifrons*	Southern Bottlenose Whale
Iniidae	*Geoffrensis*	Amazon River Dolphin
Echimyidae	*Bistriata*	Yellow-crowned Brush-tailed Rat
Echimyidae	*Pagurus*	Plain Brush-tailed Rat
Cricetidae	*Pictipes*	Lesser Wilfred's Mouse
Cricetidae	*Rimofrons*	Cleft-headed Juliomys
Cricetidae	*Candango*	Candango Mouse
Echimyidae	*Amblyonyx*	Atlantic Bamboo Rat
Caviidae	*Rupestris*	Rock Cavy
Physeteridae	*Breviceps*	Pygmy Sperm Whale
Physeteridae	*Sima*	Dwarf Sperm Whale
Cricetidae	*Fronto*	Fossorial Giant Rat
Cricetidae	*Tomentosus*	Woolly Giant Rat
Phyllostomidae	*Brachyotis*	Orange-throated Bat
Vespertilionidae	*Blossevillii*	Red Bat
Vespertilionidae	*Ega*	Southern Yellow Bat
Vespertilionidae	*Egregius*	Big Red Bat
Callitrichidae	*Caissara*	Black-faced Lion Tamarin
Callitrichidae	*Chrysomelas*	Golden-headed Lion Tamarin
Callitrichidae	*Chrysopygus*	Black Lion Tamarin
Callitrichidae	*Rosalia*	Golden Lion Tamarin
Felidae	*Colocolo*	Pampas Cat
Felidae	*Geoffroyi*	Geoffroy's Cat
Felidae	*Pardalis*	Ocelot
Felidae	*Tigrinus*	Oncilla
Felidae	*Wiedii*	Margay
Phyllostomidae	*Obscura*	Dark Long-tongued Bat
Phyllostomidae	*Spurrelli*	Chestnut Long-tongued Bat
Delphinidae	*Peronii*	Southern Right Whale Dolphin
Phyllostomidae	*Bokermanni*	Bokermann's Nectar Bat
Phyllostomidae	*Dekeyseri*	Dekeyser's Nectar Bat
Phyllostomidae	*Mordax* ·	Goldman' Nectar Bat

Family	Species	Common names (Eng)
Phyllostomidae	*Thomasi*	Thomas's Nectar Bat
Phyllostomidae	*Aurita*	Common Sword-nosed Bat
Mustelidae	*Longicaudis*	Long-tailed Otter
Phyllostomidae	*Brasiliense*	Pygmy Round-eared Bat
Phyllostomidae	*Carrikeri*	Carriker's Round-eared Bat
Phyllostomidae	*Schulzi*	Schultz's Round-eared Bat
Phyllostomidae	*Silvicolum*	White-throated Round-eared Bat
Didelphidae	*Crassicaudata*	Little Water Opossum
Phyllostomidae	*Macrophyllum*	Long-legged Bat
Echimyidae	*Didelphoides*	Brazilian Spiny Tree Rat
Echimyidae	*Macrura*	Long-tailed Tree Rat
Echimyidae	*Obscura*	Dark Armored Tree-rat
Didelphidae	*Noctivagus*	White-bellied Slender Mouse Opossum
Didelphidae	*Parvidens*	Delicate Slender Mouse Opossum
Didelphidae	*Paulensis*	Brazilian Slender Opossum
Didelphidae	*Pinheiroi*	Pinheiro's Slender Opossum
Cervidae	*Americana*	Red Brocket
Cervidae	*Bororo*	Small Red Brocket
Cervidae	*Gouazoubira*	Gray Brocket
Cervidae	*Nana*	Brazilian Dwarf Brocket
Cervidae	*Nemorivaga*	Amazonian Brown Brocket Deer
Ziphiidae	*Densirostris*	Blainville's Beaked Whale
Ziphiidae	*Europaeus*	Gervais' Beaked Whale
Ziphiidae	*Grayi*	Gray's Beaked Whale
Ziphiidae	*Hectori*	Hector's Beaked Whale
Ziphiidae	*Layardii*	Strap-toothed Whale
Ziphiidae	*Mirus*	True's Beaked Whale
Didelphidae	*Nudicaudatus*	Brown Four-eyed Opossum
Callitrichidae	*Acariensis*	Rio Acarí Marmoset
Callitrichidae	*Argentatus*	Silvery Marmoset
Callitrichidae	*Manicorensis*	Manicoré Marmoset
Callitrichidae	*Mauesi*	Maués Marmoset
Callitrichidae	*Melanurus*	Black-tailed Marmoset
Callitrichidae	*Nigriceps*	Black-headed Marmoset
Callitrichidae	*Saterei*	Sateré Marmoset
Cricetidae	*Transitorius*	Transitional Colilargo
Phyllostomidae	*Hirsuta*	Hairy Big-eared Bat
Phyllostomidae	*Megalotis*	Little Big-eared Bat
Phyllostomidae	*Microtis*	Common Big-eared Bat
Phyllostomidae	*Minuta*	White-bellied Big-eared Bat

Family	Species	Common names (Eng)
Phyllostomidae	*Schmidtorum*	Schmidts's Big-eared Bat
Sciuridae	*Flaviventer*	Amazon Dwarf Squirrel
Phyllostomidae	*Bennettii*	Golden Bat
Phyllostomidae	*Crenulatum*	Striped Hairy-nosed Bat
Molossidae	*Mattogrossensis*	Mato Grosso Dog-faced Bat
Molossidae	*Neglectus*	Rufous Dog-faced Bat
Molossidac	*Rufus*	Black Mastiff Bat
Didelphidae	*Scalops*	Long-nosed Short-tailed Opossum
Didelphidae	*Sorex*	Hensel´s Short-tailed Opossum
Didelphidae	*Theresa*	Southern Three-striped Opossum
Mustelidae	*Africana*	Amazon Weasel
Mustelidae	*Frenata*	Long-tailed Weasel
Myocastoridae	*Coypus*	Coypu
Dasyproctidae	*Acouchy*	Red Acouchi
Dasyproctidae	*Pratti*	Green Acouchi
Vespertilionidae	*Albescens*	Silver-tipped Myotis
Vespertilionidae	*Levis*	Yellowish Myotis
Vespertilionidae	*Riparius*	Riparian Myotis
Vespertilionidae	*Ruber*	Red Myotis
Vespertilionidae	*Simus*	Velvety Myotis
Myrmecophagidae	*Tridactyla*	Giant Anteater
Procyonidae	*Nasua*	South American Coati
Cricetidae	*Lasiurus*	Hairy-tailed Bolo Mouse
Cricetidae	*Urichi*	Northern Grass Mouse
Cricetidae	*Rattus*	Amazonian Mouse
Cricetidae	*Squamipes*	South American Water Rat
Phyllostomidae	*Pusilla*	Least Big-eared Bat
Cricetidae	*Oyapocki*	Oyapock's Fish-eating Rat
Noctilionidae	*Albiventris*	Lesser Bulldog Bat
Noctilionidae	*Leporinus*	Greater Bulldog Bat
Cricetidae	*Edwardsii*	Edwards's Long-clawed Mouse
Molossidae	*Aurispinosus*	Peale's Free-tailed Bat
Molossidae	*Laticaudatus*	Broad-eared Bat
Molossidae	*Macrotis*	Big Free-tailed Bat
Cervidae	*Virginianus*	White-tailed Deer
Cricetidae	*Bicolor*	Bicolored Arboreal Rice Rat
Cricetidae	*Roberti*	Robert's Arboreal Rice Rat
Cricetidae	*Rutilus*	Red Arboreal Rice Rat
Cricetidae	*Superans*	Foothill Arboreal Rice Rat
Cricetidae	*Trinitatis*	Long-furred Rice Rat

Family	Species	Common names (Eng)
Cricetidae	*Chacoensis*	Chacoan Pygmy Rice Rat
Cricetidae	*Angularis*	Angular Hocicudo
Cricetidae	*Delator*	Spy Hocicudo
Cricetidae	*Hispidus*	Hispid Hocicudo
Cricetidae	*Nasutus*	Long-nosed Hocicudo
Cricetidae	*Roberti*	Robert's Hocicudo
Cervidae	*Bezoarticus*	Pampas Deer
Felidae	*Onca*	Jaguar
Tayassuidae	*Maximus*	Giant Peccary
Tayassuidae	*Tajacu*	Collared Peccary
Delphinidae	*Electra*	Melon-headed Whale
Emballonuridae	*Kappleri*	Greater Dog-like Bat
Emballonuridae	*Leucoptera*	White-winged Dog-like Bat
Emballonuridae	*Macrotis*	Lesser Dog-like Bat
Cricetidae	*Ferrugineus*	Rio De Janeiro Arboreal Rat
Didelphidae	*Opossum*	Gray Four-eyed Opossum
Phyllostomidae	*Stenops*	Pale-faced Bat
Echimyidae	*Blainvillii*	Golden Atlantic Tree Rat
Echimyidae	*Brasiliensis*	Red-nosed Tree Rat
Echimyidae	*Dasythrix*	Drab Atlantic Tree Rat
Phyllostomidae	*Discolor*	Pale Spear-nosed Bat
Phyllostomidae	*Elongatus*	Lesser Spear-nosed Bat
Phyllostomidae	*Hastatus*	Greater Spear-nosed Bat
Phyllostomidae	*Latifolius*	Guianan Spear-nosed Bat
Pitheciidae	*Albicans*	White Saki
Pitheciidae	*Monachus*	Geoffroy's Monk Saki
Pitheciidae	*Pithecia*	Golden-faced Saki
Phyllostomidae	*Brachycephalus*	Short-headed Broad-nosed Bat
Phyllostomidae	*Helleri*	Heller's Broad-nosed Bat
Phyllostomidae	*Infuscus*	Buffy Broad-nosed Bat
Phyllostomidae	*Lineatus*	White-lined Bat
Phyllostomidae	*Recifinus*	Recife Broad-nosed Bat
Iniidae	*Blainvillei*	Franciscana
Procyonidae	*Flavus*	Kinkajou
Dasypodidae	*Maximus*	Giant Armadillo
Procyonidae	*Cancrivorus*	Crab-eating Raccoon
Molossidae	*Centralis*	Big Crested Mastiff Bat
Molossidae	*Nasutus*	Brown Mastiff Bat
Canidae	*Vetulus*	Hoary Fox
Cricetidae	*Simplex*	Brazilian False Rice Rat

Family	Species	Common names (Eng)
Mormoopidae	*Gymnonotus*	Big Naked-backed Bat
Mustelidae	*Brasiliensis*	Giant Brazilian Otter
Felidae	*Concolor*	Puma
Felidae	*Yagouaroundi*	Jaguarundi
Cricetidae	*Rufescens*	Brazilian Arboreal Mouse
Phyllostomidae	*Fischerae*	Fischer's Little Fruit Bat
Phyllostomidae	*Pumilio*	Dwarf Little Fruit Bat
Cricetidae	*Leucodactylus*	White-footed Climbing Mouse
Vespertilionidae	*Hussoni*	Husson's Yellow Bat
Vespertilionidae	*Io*	Thomas's Yellow Bat
Emballonuridae	*Naso*	Proboscis Bat
Emballonuridae	*Bilineata*	Greater Sac-winged Bat
Emballonuridae	*Canescens*	Frosted Sac-winged Bat
Emballonuridae	*Gymnura*	Amazonian Sac-winged Bat
Emballonuridae	*Leptura*	Lesser Sac-winged Bat
Callitrichidae	*Bicolor*	Brazilian Bare-faced Tamarin
Callitrichidae	*Fuscicollis*	Saddleback Tamarin
Callitrichidae	*Midas*	Golden-handed Tamarin
Callitrichidae	*Mystax*	Moustached Tamarin
Callitrichidae	*Niger*	Black-handed Tamarin
Callitrichidae	*Nigricollis*	Black Mantle Tamarin
Cebidae	*Ustus*	Golden-backed Squirrel Monkey
Sciuridae	*Aestuans*	Guianan Squirrel
Sciuridae	*Gilvigularis*	Yellow-throated Squirrel
Sciuridae	*Igniventris*	Northern Amazon Red Squirrel
Sciuridae	*Spadiceus*	Southern Amazon Red Squirrel
Phyllostomidae	*Ega*	Ega Long-tongued Bat
Cricetidae	*Ucayalensis*	Ucayali Spiny Mouse
Cricetidae	*Alstoni*	Alston's Cotton Rat
Erethizontidae	*Villosus*	Orange-spined Hairy Dwarf Porcupine
Delphinidae	*Attenuata*	Pantropical Spotted Dolphin
Delphinidae	*Clymene*	Clymene Dolphin
Delphinidae	*Coeruleoalba*	Striped Dolphin
Delphinidae	*Frontalis*	Atlantic Spotted Dolphin
Delphinidae	*Longirostris*	Spinner Dolphin
Delphinidae	*Bredanensis*	Rough-toothed Dolphin
Molossidae	*Brasiliensis*	Brazilian Free-tailed Bat
Myrmecophagidae	*Tetradactyla*	Lesser Anteater
Tapiridae	*Terrestris*	Brazilian Tapir
Tayassuidae	*Pecari*	White-lipped Peccary

Family	Species	Common names (Eng)
Cricetidae	*Cerradensis*	Cerrado Mouse
Cricetidae	*Lasiotis*	Hairy-eared Cerrado Mouse
Cricetidae	*Nigrita*	Blackish Grass Mouse
Echimyidae	*Apereoides*	Punare
Thyropteridae	*Discifera*	Peter's Disk-winged Bat
Thyropteridae	*Tricolor*	Spix's Disk-winged Bat
Dasypodidae	*Matacus*	Southern Three-banded Armadillo
Dasypodidae	*Tricinctus*	Brazilian Three-banded Armadillo
Phyllostomidae	*Bidens*	Greater Round-eared Bat
Phyllostomidae	*Saurophila*	Stripe-headed Round-eared Bat
Echimyidae	*Grandis*	Giant Tree Rat
Phyllostomidae	*Cirrhosus*	Fringe-lipped Bat
Trichechidae	*Inunguis*	Amazonian Manatee
Delphinidae	*Truncatus*	Common Bottlenose Dolphin
Phyllostomidae	*Bilobatum*	Tent-maiking Bat
Phyllostomidae	*Magnirostrum*	Brown Tent-making Bat
Phyllostomidae	*Bidens*	Bedentate Yellow-eared Bat
Phyllostomidae	*Brocki*	Brock's Yellow-eared Bat
Phyllostomidae	*Pusilla*	Little Yellow-eared Bat
Phyllostomidae	*Thyone*	Northern Little Yellow-eared Bat
Phyllostomidae	*Caraccioli*	Great Stripe-faced Bat
Phyllostomidae	*Spectrum*	Spectral Bat
Cricetidae	*Pyrrhorhinos*	Red-nosed Mouse
Cricetidae	*Oenax*	Greater Wilfred's Mouse
Cricetidae	*Brevicauda*	Short-tailed Cane Mouse

Family	Species	Common names (Eng)
Accipitridae	Bicolor	Bicoloured Hawk
Accipitridae	Poliogaster	Gray-bellied Hawk
Accipitridae	Striatus	Sharp-shinned Hawk
Accipitridae	Superciliosus	Tiny Hawk
Furnariidae	Fonsecai	Pink-legged Graveteiro
Scolopacidae	Macularius	Spotted Sandpiper
Strigidae	Harrisii	Buff-fronted Owl
Apodidae	Montivagus	White-tipped Swift
Ardeidae	Agami	Agami Heron
Icteridae	Badius	Bay-winged Cowbird
Icteridae	Cyanopus	Unicoloured Blackbird
Icteridae	Thilius	Yellow-winged Blackbird
Tyrannidae	Risora	Strange-tailed Tyrant
Tyrannidae	Tricolor	Cock-tailed Tyrant
Psittacidae	Xanthops	Yellow-faced Parrot
Hirundinidae	Fucata	Tawny-headed Swallow
Rallidae	Concolor	Uniform Crake
Emberizidae	Moesta	Blackish-blue Seedeater
Trochilidae	Brevirostris	White-chested Emerald
Trochilidae	Chionogaster	White-bellied Hummingbird
Trochilidae	Fimbriata	Glittering-throated Emerald
Trochilidae	Lactea	Sapphire-spangled Emerald
Trochilidae	Leucogaster	Plain-bellied Emerald
Trochilidae	Versicolor	Versicoloured Emerald
Trochilidae	Viridigaster	Green-bellied Hummingbird
Psittacidae	Aestiva	Blue-fronted Parrot
Psittacidae	Autumnalis	Red-lored Parrot
Psittacidae	Brasiliensis	Red-tailed Parrot
Psittacidae	Farinosa	Mealy Parrot
Psittacidae	Festiva	Festive Parrot
Psittacidae	Kawalli	Kawall's Parrot
Psittacidae	Ochrocephala	Yellow-crowned Parrot
Psittacidae	Pretrei	Red-spectacled Parrot
Psittacidae	Rhodocorytha	Red-browed Parrot
Psittacidae	Vinacea	Vinaceous Parrot
Anatidae	Brasiliensis	Brazilian Teal
Icteridae	Holosericeus	Scarlet-headed Blackbird
Emberizidae	Aurifrons	Yellow-browed Sparrow
Emberizidae	Humeralis	Grassland Sparrow
Furnariidae	Amaurotis	White-browed Foliage-gleaner

Family	Species	Common names (Eng)
Furnariidae	Dorsalis	Dusky-cheeked Foliage-gleaner
Furnariidae	Fuscus	White-collared Foliage-gleaner
Anatidae	Bahamensis	White-cheeked Pintail
Anatidae	Cyanoptera	Cinnamon Teal
Anatidae	Discors	Blue-winged Teal
Anatidae	Flavirostris	Speckled Teal
Anatidae	Georgica	Yellow-billed Pintail
Anatidae	Platalea	Red Shoveler
Anatidae	Sibilatrix	Chiloe Wigeon
Anatidae	Versicolor	Silver Teal
Furnariidae	Strigilatus	Chestnut-winged Hookbill
Anhimidae	Cornuta	Horned Screamer
Anhingidae	Anhinga	Anhinga
Psittacidae	Glaucus	Glaucous Macaw
Psittacidae	Hyacinthinus	Hyacinth Macaw
Psittacidae	Leari	Lear's Macaw, Indigo Macaw
Trochilidae	Gounellei	Broad-tipped Hermit
Laridae	Minutus	Black Noddy
Laridae	Stolidus	Brown Noddy
Trochilidae	Nigricollis	Black-throated Mango
Trochilidae	Viridigula	Green-throated Mango
Motacillidae	Correndera	Correndera Pipit
Motacillidae	Nattereri	Ochre-breasted Pipit
Pipridae	Bokermanni	Araripe Manakin
Pipridae	Galeata	Helmeted Manakin
Furnariidae	Annumbi	Firewood-gatherer
Rallidae	Castaneiceps	Chestnut-headed Crake
Rallidae	Fasciatus	Black-banded Crake
Rallidae	Viridis	Russet-crowned Crake
Trochilidae	Cirrochloris	Sombre Hummingbird
Psittacidae	Ararauna	Blue-and-yellow Macaw
Psittacidae	Chloropterus	Red-and-green Macaw
Psittacidae	Macao	Scarlet Macaw
Psittacidae	Severus	Chestnut-fronted Macaw
Rallidae	Cajanea	Grey-necked Wood-rail
Rallidae	Calopterus	Red-winged Wood-rail
Rallidae	Mangle	Little Wood-rail
Rallidae	Saracura	Slaty-breasted Wood-rail
Rallidae	Ypecaha	Giant Wood-rail
Aramidae	Guarauna	Limpkin

Family	Species	Common names (Eng)
Psittacidae	*Acuticaudata*	Blue-crowned Parakeet
Psittacidae	*Aurea*	Peach-fronted Parakeet
Psittacidae	*Auricapillus*	Golden-capped Parakeet
Psittacidae	*Cactorum*	Cactus Parakeet
Psittacidae	*Jandaya*	Jandaya Parakeet
Psittacidae	*Leucophthalma*	White-eyed Parakeet
Psittacidae	*Pertinax*	Brown-throated Parakeet
Psittacidae	*Solstitialis*	Sun Parakeet
Psittacidae	*Weddellii*	Dusky-headed Parakeet
Ardeidae	*Cinerea*	Grey Heron
Ardeidae	*Cocoi*	Cocoi Heron
Scolopacidae	*Interpres*	Ruddy Turnstone
Emberizidae	*Flavirostris*	Saffron-billed Sparrow
Emberizidae	*Taciturnus*	Pectoral Sparrow
Emberizidae	*Conirostris*	Black-striped Sparrow
Tyrannidae	*Leucocephala*	White-headed Marsh-tyrant
Strigidae	*Flammeus*	Short-eared Owl
Strigidae	*Stygius*	Stygian Owl
Furnariidae	*Baeri*	Short-billed Canastero
Furnariidae	*Hudsoni*	Hudson's Canastero
Furnariidae	*Luizae*	Cipó Canastero
Tyrannidae	*Pilaris*	Pale-eyed Pygmy-tyrant
Strigidae	*Cunicularia*	Burrowing Owl
Emberizidae	*Personatus*	Tepui Brush-finch
Hirundinidae	*Fasciata*	White-banded Swallow
Hirundinidae	*Melanoleuca*	Black-collared Swallow
Tyrannidae	*Citriniventris*	Citron-bellied Attila
Tyrannidae	*Phoenicurus*	Rufous-tailed Attila
Trochilidae	*Lumachella*	Hooded Visorbearer
Trochilidae	*Scutatus*	Hyacinth Visorbearer
Ramphastidae	*Derbianus*	Chestnut-tipped Toucanet
Ramphastidae	*Prasinus*	Emerald Toucanet
Furnariidae	*Infuscatus*	Olive-backed Foliage-gleaner
Furnariidae	*Leucophthalmus*	White-eyed Foliage-gleaner
Furnariidae	*Rubiginosus*	Ruddy Foliage-gleaner
Furnariidae	*Rufipileatus*	Chestnut-crowned Foliage-gleaner
Trochilidae	*Recurvirostris*	Fiery-tailed Awlbill
Scolopacidae	*Longicauda*	Upland Sandpiper
Momotidae	*Martii*	Rufous Motmot
Momotidae	*Ruficapillus*	Rufous-capped Motmot

Family	Species	Common names (Eng)
Parulidae	*Bivittatus*	Two-banded Warbler
Parulidae	*Culicivorus*	Golden-crowned Warbler
Parulidae	*Flaveolus*	Flavescent Warbler
Parulidae	*Hypoleucus*	White-bellied Warbler
Thamnophilidae	*Cinerea*	Giant Antshrike
Furnariidae	*Rikeri*	Point-tailed Palmcreeper
Thamnophilidae	*Nigropectus*	White-bearded Antshrike
Ardeidae	*Pinnatus*	Pinnated Bittern
Galbulidae	*Albogularis*	White-throated Jacamar
Galbulidae	*Lugubris*	Brown Jacamar
Psittacidae	*Chiriri*	Yellow-chevroned Parakeet
Psittacidae	*Chrysoptera*	Golden-winged Parakeet
Psittacidae	*Sanctithomae*	Tui Parakeet
Psittacidae	*Tirica*	Plain Parakeet
Psittacidae	*Versicolurus*	White-winged Parakeet
Strigidae	*Virginianus*	Great Horned Owl
Ardeidae	*Ibis*	Cattle Egret
Bucconidae	*Capensis*	Collared Puffbird
Bucconidae	*Macrodactylus*	Chestnut-capped Puffbird
Bucconidae	*Tamatia*	Spotted Puffbird
Burhinidae	*Bistriatus*	Double-striped Thick-knee
Accipitridae	*Nigricollis*	Black-collared Hawk
Accipitridae	*Albicaudatus*	White-tailed Hawk
Accipitridae	*Brachyurus*	Short-tailed Hawk
Accipitridae	*Leucorrhous*	White-rumped Hawk
Accipitridae	*Magnirostris*	Roadside Hawk
Accipitridae	*Nitidus*	Grey Hawk
Accipitridae	*Platypterus*	Broad-winged Hawk
Accipitridae	*Swainsoni*	Swainson's Hawk
Accipitridae	*Aequinoctialis*	Rufous Crab-hawk
Accipitridae	*Meridionalis*	Savanna Hawk
Accipitridae	*Urubitinga*	Great Black-hawk
Ardeidae	*Striata*	Striated Heron
Icteridae	*Cela*	Yellow-rumped Cacique
Icteridae	*Chrysopterus*	Golden-winged Cacique
Anatidae	*Moschata*	Muscovy Duck
Scolopacidae	*Alba*	Sanderling
Scolopacidae	*Bairdii*	Baird's Sandpiper
Scolopacidae	*Canutus*	Red Knot
Scolopacidae	*Fuscicollis*	White-rumped Sandpiper

Family	Species	Common names (Eng)
Scolopacidae	*Himantopus*	Stilt Sandpiper
Scolopacidae	*Melanotos*	Pectoral Sandpiper
Scolopacidae	*Minutilla*	Least Sandpiper
Scolopacidae	*Pusilla*	Semipalmated Sandpiper
Trochilidae	*Amethystina*	Amethyst Woodstar
Anatidae	*Leucophrys*	Ringed Teal
Procellariidae	*Diomedea*	Cory's Shearwater
Cotingidae	*Cristata*	Kinglet Calyptura
Picidae	*Leucopogon*	Cream-backed Woodpecker
Picidae	*Melanoleucos*	Crimson-crested Woodpecker
Picidae	*Robustus*	Robust Woodpecker
Picidae	*Rubricollis*	Red-necked Woodpecker
Tyrannidae	*Obsoletum*	Southern Beardless-tyrannulet
Trochilidae	*Duidae*	Buff-breasted Sabrewing
Trochilidae	*Hyperythrus*	Rufous-breasted Sabrewing
Trochilidae	*Largipennis*	Grey-breasted Sabrewing
Dendrocolaptidae	*Falcularius*	Black-billed Scythebill
Troglodytidae	*Griseus*	Bicoloured Wren
Troglodytidae	*Turdinus*	Thrush-like Wren
Ramphastidae	*Auratus*	Gilded Barbet
Ramphastidae	*Aurovirens*	Scarlet-crowned Barbet
Ramphastidae	*Brunneipectus*	Brown-chested Barbet
Ramphastidae	*Dayi*	Black-girdled Barbet
Ramphastidae	*Niger*	Black-spotted Barbet
Caprimulgidae	*Cayennensis*	White-tailed Nightjar
Caprimulgidae	*Hirundinaceus*	Pygmy Nightjar
Caprimulgidae	*Longirostris*	Band-winged Nightjar
Caprimulgidae	*Maculicaudus*	Spot-tailed Nightjar
Caprimulgidae	*Rufus*	Rufous Nightjar
Caprimulgidae	*Sericocaudatus*	Silky-tailed Nightjar
Caprimulgidae	*Whitelyi*	Roraiman Nightjar
Tyrannidae	*Flaveola*	Yellow Tyrannulet
Falconidae	*Cheriway*	Crested Caracara
Falconidae	*Plancus*	Southern Caracara
Fringillidae	*Magellanica*	Hooded Siskin
Fringillidae	*Yarrellii*	Yellow-faced Siskin
Cariamidae	*Cristata*	Red-legged Seriema
Cotingidae	*Cucullata*	Hooded Berryeater
Cotingidae	*Melanocephala*	Black-headed Berryeater
Cardinalidae	*Canadensis*	Yellow-green Grosbeak

Family	Species	Common names (Eng)
Tyrannidae	*Fuscus*	Ash-throated Casiornis
Tyrannidae	*Rufus*	Rufous Casiornis
Ardeidae	*Albus*	Great White Egret
Emberizidae	*Homochroa*	Paramo Seedeater
Cathartidae	*Aura*	Turkey Vulture
Cathartidae	*Burrovianus*	Lesser Yellow-headed Vulture
Cathartidae	*Melambrotus*	Greater Yellow-headed Vulture
Turdidae	*Fuscescens*	Veery
Turdidae	*Minimus*	Grey-cheeked Thrush
Turdidae	*Ustulatus*	Swainson's Thrush
Scolopacidae	*Semipalmatus*	Willet
Picidae	*Elegans*	Chestnut Woodpecker
Picidae	*Flavescens*	Blond-crested Woodpecker
Picidae	*Flavus*	Cream-coloured Woodpecker
Picidae	*Grammicus*	Scaly-breasted Woodpecker
Picidae	*Spectabilis*	Rufous-headed Woodpecker
Picidae	*Torquatus*	Ringed Woodpecker
Picidae	*Undatus*	Waved Woodpecker
Cotingidae	*Ornatus*	Amazonian Umbrellabird
Threskiornithidae	*Oxycerca*	Sharp-tailed Ibis
Thamnophilidae	*Carbonaria*	Rio Branco Antbird
Thamnophilidae	*Cinerascens*	Grey Antbird
Thamnophilidae	*Ferdinandi*	Bananal Antbird
Thamnophilidae	*Laeta*	Laeta Antbird
Thamnophilidae	*Manu*	Manu Antbird
Thamnophilidae	*Melanaria*	Mato Grosso Antbird
Thamnophilidae	*Nigrescens*	Blackish Antbird
Thamnophilidae	*Nigricans*	Jet Antbird
Thamnophilidae	*Serva*	Black Antbird
Thamnophilidae	*Tyrannina*	Dusky Antbird
Furnariidae	*Cinnamomeus*	Yellow-chinned Spinetail
Furnariidae	*Mustelinus*	Red-and-white Spinetail
Apodidae	*Brachyura*	Short-tailed Swift
Apodidae	*Chapmani*	Chapman's Swift
Apodidae	*Cinereiventris*	Grey-rumped Swift
Apodidae	*Egregia*	Pale-rumped Swift
Apodidae	*Meridionalis*	Sick's Swift
Apodidae	*Pelagica*	Chimney Swift
Apodidae	*Spinicaudus*	Band-rumped Swift
Apodidae	*Viridipennis*	Amazonian Swift

Family	Species	Common names (Eng)
Formicariidae	*Campanisona*	Short-tailed Antthrush
Formicariidae	*Ruficauda*	Rufous-tailed Antthrush
Charadriidae	*Collaris*	Collared Plover
Charadriidae	*Falklandicus*	Two-banded Plover
Charadriidae	*Modestus*	Rufous-chested Plover
Charadriidae	*Semipalmatus*	Semipalmated Plover
Charadriidae	*Wilsonia*	Wilson's Plover
Emberizidae	*Eucosma*	Coal-crested Finch
Anhimidae	*Torquata*	Southern Screamer
Bucconidae	*Tenebrosa*	Swallow-wing
Pipridae	*Caudata*	Swallow-tailed Manakin
Pipridae	*Pareola*	Blue-backed Manakin
Laridae	*Niger*	Black Tern
Trochilidae	*Notata*	Blue-chinned Sapphire
Alcedinidae	*Amazona*	Amazon Kingfisher
Alcedinidae	*Americana*	Green Kingfisher
Alcedinidae	*Inda*	Green-and-rufous Kingfisher
Thraupidae	*Spiza*	Green Honeycreeper
Thraupidae	*Cyanea*	Blue-naped Chlorophonia
Trochilidae	*Lucidus*	Glittering-bellied Emerald
Trochilidae	*Mellisugus*	Blue-tailed Emerald
Accipitridae	*Uncinatus*	Hook-billed Kite
Caprimulgidae	*Acutipennis*	Lesser Nighthawk
Caprimulgidae	*Minor*	Common Nighthawk
Caprimulgidae	*Pusillus*	Least Nighthawk
Caprimulgidae	*Rupestris*	Sand-coloured Nighthawk
Trochilidae	*Mosquitus*	Ruby-topaz Hummingbird
Icteridae	*Icterocephalus*	Yellow-hooded Blackbird
Icteridae	*Ruficapillus*	Chestnut-capped Blackbird
Trochilidae	*Oenone*	Golden-tailed Sapphire
Furnariidae	*Leucophrus*	Pale-browed Treehunter
Turdidae	*Leucogenys*	Rufous-brown Solitaire
Ciconiidae	*Maguari*	Maguari Stork
Furnariidae	*Fuscus*	Bar-winged Cinclodes
Furnariidae	*Pabsti*	Long-tailed Cinclodes
Accipitridae	*Buffoni*	Long-winged Harrier
Accipitridae	*Cinereus*	Cinereous Harrier
Thraupidae	*Leverianus*	Magpie Tanager
Troglodytidae	*Platensis*	Sedge Wren, Grass Wren
Columbidae	*Godefrida*	Purple-winged Ground-dove

Family	Species	Common names (Eng)
Columbidae	*Pretiosa*	Blue Ground-dove
Icteridae	*Oseryi*	Casqued Oropendola
Thamnophilidae	*Atrogularis*	Rondonia Bushbird
Trochilidae	*Rubricauda*	Brazilian Ruby
Tyrannidae	*Fuscatus*	Fuscous Flycatcher
Tyrannidae	*Subbrunneus*	Brownish Flycatcher
Tyrannidae	*Superrufus*	Rufous Twistwing
Cuculidae	*Cinerea*	Ash-coloured Cuckoo
Cuculidae	*Minuta*	Little Cuckoo
Cuculidae	*Pumila*	Dwarf Cuckoo
Cuculidae	*Americanus*	Yellow-billed Cuckoo
Cuculidae	*Erythropthalmus*	Black-billed Cuckoo
Cuculidae	*Euleri*	Pearly-breasted Cuckoo
Cuculidae	*Melacoryphus*	Dark-billed Cuckoo
Cuculidae	*Minor*	Mangrove Cuckoo
Ardeidae	*Cochlearius*	Boat-billed Heron
Coerebidae	*Flaveola*	Bananaquit
Picidae	*Campestris*	Campo Flicker
Picidae	*Melanochloros*	Green-barred Woodpecker
Picidae	*Punctigula*	Spot-breasted Woodpecker
Picidae	*Rubiginosus*	Golden-olive Woodpecker
Trochilidae	*Coruscans*	Sparkling Violet-ear
Trochilidae	*Delphinae*	Brown Violet-ear
Trochilidae	*Serrirostris*	White-vented Violet-ear
Odontophoridae	*Cristatus*	Crested Bobwhite
Tyrannidae	*Colonus*	Long-tailed Tyrant
Columbidae	*Cyanopis*	Blue-eyed Ground-dove
Columbidae	*Minuta*	Plain-breasted Ground-dove
Columbidae	*Passerina*	Common Ground-dove
Columbidae	*Picui*	Picui Ground-dove
Columbidae	*Squammata*	Scaled Dove
Columbidae	*Talpacoti*	Ruddy Ground-dove
Thraupidae	*Loricata*	Scarlet-throated Tanager
Cotingidae	*Mcilhennyi*	Black-faced Cotinga
Thraupidae	*Bicolor*	Bicoloured Conebill
Thraupidae	*Margaritae*	Pearly-breasted Conebill
Thraupidae	*Speciosum*	Chestnut-vented Conebill
Tyrannidae	*Parvus*	Yellow-throated Flycatcher
Tyrannidae	*Trivirgatus*	Three-striped Flycatcher
Conopophagidae	*Aurita*	Chestnut-belted Gnateater

Family	Species	Common names (Eng)
Conopophagidae	*Lineata*	Rufous Gnateater
Conopophagidae	*Melanogaster*	Black-bellied Gnateater
Conopophagidae	*Melanops*	Black-cheeked Gnateater
Conopophagidae	*Peruviana*	Ash-throated Gnateater
Conopophagidae	*Roberti*	Hooded Gnateater
Thraupidae	*Mesoleuca*	Cone-billed Tanager
Thraupidae	*Speculigera*	Black-and-white Tanager
Tyrannidae	*Albogularis*	White-throated Pewee
Tyrannidae	*Cinereus*	Tropical Pewee
Tyrannidae	*Cooperi*	Olive-sided Flycatcher
Tyrannidae	*Fumigatus*	Smoke-coloured Pewee
Tyrannidae	*Nigrescens*	Blackish Pewee
Tyrannidae	*Sordidulus*	Western Wood-pewee
Tyrannidae	*Virens*	Eastern Wood-pewee
Cathartidae	*Atratus*	Black Vulture
Pipridae	*Gutturalis*	White-throated Manakin
Emberizidae	*Melanotis*	Black-masked Finch
Furnariidae	*Alaudina*	Lark-like Brushrunner
Emberizidae	*Cucullatus*	Red-crested Finch
Emberizidae	*Pileatus*	Pileated Finch
Tyrannidae	*Delalandi*	Southern Antpipit
Tyrannidae	*Torquatus*	Ringed Antpipit
Anatidae	*Coscoroba*	Coscoroba Swan
Cotingidae	*Cayana*	Spangled Cotinga
Cotingidae	*Cotinga*	Purple-breasted Cotinga
Cotingidae	*Maculata*	Banded Cotinga
Cotingidae	*Maynana*	Plum-throated Cotinga
Rallidae	*Notatus*	Speckled Rail
Furnariidae	*Demissa*	Tepui Spinetail
Furnariidae	*Gutturata*	Speckled Spinetail
Furnariidae	*Muelleri*	Scaled Spinetail
Furnariidae	*Obsoleta*	Olive Spinetail
Furnariidae	*Pallida*	Pallid Spinetail
Furnariidae	*Pyrrhophia*	Stripe-crowned Spinetail
Furnariidae	*Semicinerea*	Grey-headed Spinetail
Furnariidae	*Sulphurifera*	Sulphur-throated Spinetail
Furnariidae	*Vulpecula*	Parker's Spinetail
Cracidae	*Globulosa*	Wattled Curassow
Cuculidae	*Ani*	Smooth-billed Ani
Cuculidae	*Major*	Greater Ani

Family	Species	Common names (Eng)
Cuculidae	*Sulcirostris*	Groove-billed Ani
Tinamidae	*Atrocapillus*	Black-capped Tinamou
Tinamidae	*Bartletti*	Bartlett's Tinamou
Tinamidae	*Brevirostris*	Rusty Tinamou
Tinamidae	*Cinereus*	Cinereous Tinamou
Tinamidae	*Obsoletus*	Brown Tinamou
Tinamidae	*Parvirostris*	Small-billed Tinamou
Tinamidae	*Soui*	Little Tinamou
Tinamidae	*Strigulosus*	Brazilian Tinamou
Tinamidae	*Tataupa*	Tataupa Tinamou
Tyrannidae	*Caudacuta*	Sharp-tailed Tyrant
Icteridae	*Forbesi*	Forbes's Blackbird
Thraupidae	*Caeruleus*	Purple Honeycreeper
Thraupidae	*Cyaneus*	Red-legged Honeycreeper
Thraupidae	*Nitidus*	Short-billed Honeycreeper
Thraupidae	*Cyanicterus*	Blue-backed Tanager
Cardinalidae	*Brissonii*	Ultramarine Grosbeak
Cardinalidae	*Cyanoides*	Blue-black Grosbeak
Corvidae	*Caeruleus*	Azure Jay
Corvidae	*Cayanus*	Cayenne Jay
Corvidae	*Chrysops*	Plush-crested Jay
Corvidae	*Cristatellus*	Curl-crested Jay
Corvidae	*Cyanomelas*	Purplish Jay
Corvidae	*Cyanopogon*	White-naped Jay
Corvidae	*Heilprini*	Azure-naped Jay
Corvidae	*Violaceus*	Violaceous Jay
Cardinalidae	*Glaucocaerulea*	Glaucous-blue Grosbeak
Psittacidae	*Spixii*	Spix's Macaw
Vireonidae	*Gujanensis*	Rufous-browed Peppershrike
Anatidae	*Melancoryphus*	Black-necked Swan
Thamnophilidae	*Lineatus*	Fasciated Antshrike
Thamnophilidae	*Sanctaemariae*	Bamboo Antshrike
Troglodytidae	*Arada*	Musician Wren
Apodidae	*Fumigatus*	Sooty Swift
Apodidae	*Senex*	Great Dusky Swift
Thraupidae	*Hirundinacea*	White-rumped Tanager
Thraupidae	*Albiventris*	White-bellied Dacnis
Thraupidae	*Cayana*	Blue Dacnis
Thraupidae	*Flaviventer*	Yellow-bellied Dacnis
Thraupidae	*Lineata*	Black-faced Dacnis

Family	Species	Common names (Eng)
Thraupidae	*Nigripes*	Black-legged Dacnis
Procellariidae	*Capense*	Cape Petrel
Falconidae	*Ater*	Black Caracara
Dendrocolaptidae	*Longicauda*	Long-tailed Woodcreeper
Dendrocolaptidae	*Stictolaema*	Spot-throated Woodcreeper
Dendrocolaptidae	*Rufigula*	Cinnamon-throated Woodcreeper
Dendrocolaptidae	*Fuliginosa*	Plain-brown Woodcreeper
Dendrocolaptidae	*Merula*	White-chinned Woodcreeper
Dendrocolaptidae	*Certhia*	Amazonian Barred Woodcreeper
Anatidae	*Autumnalis*	Black-bellied Whistling-duck
Anatidae	*Bicolor*	Fulvous Whistling-duck
Anatidae	*Viduata*	White-faced Whistling-duck
Parulidae	*Fusca*	Blackburnian Warbler
Parulidae	*Petechia*	Yellow Warbler
Parulidae	*Striata*	Blackpoll Warbler
Dendrocolaptidae	*Kienerii*	Zimmer's Woodcreeper
Psittacidae	*Accipitrinus*	Red-fan Parrot
Thamnophilidae	*Cincta*	Banded Antbird
Thraupidae	*Duidae*	Scaled Flowerpiercer
Thraupidae	*Major*	Greater Flowerpiercer
Psittacidae	*Nobilis*	Red-shouldered Macaw
Trochilidae	*Langsdorffi*	Black-bellied Thorntail
Trochilidae	*Longicaudus*	Racket-tailed Coquette
Emberizidae	*Diuca*	Common Diuca-finch
Icteridae	*Oryzivorus*	Bobolink
Emberizidae	*Fringilloides*	White-naped Seedeater
Mimidae	*Atricapilla*	Black-capped Donacobius
Emberizidae	*Albifrons*	Long-tailed Reed-finch
Trochilidae	*Johannae*	Blue-fronted Lancebill
Cuculidae	*Pavoninus*	Pavonine Cuckoo
Cuculidae	*Phasianellus*	Pheasant Cuckoo
Thamnophilidae	*Devillei*	Striated Antbird
Thamnophilidae	*Ferruginea*	Ferruginous Antbird
Thamnophilidae	*Genei*	Rufous-tailed Antbird
Thamnophilidae	*Malura*	Dusky-tailed Antbird
Thamnophilidae	*Ochropyga*	Ochre-rumped Antbird
Thamnophilidae	*Rubricollis*	Bertoni's Antbird
Thamnophilidae	*Squamata*	Scaled Antbird
Dendrocolaptidae	*Bridgesii*	Scimitar-billed Woodcreeper
Picidae	*Galeatus*	Helmeted Woodpecker

Family	Species	Common names (Eng)
Picidae	*Lineatus*	Lineated Woodpecker
Ardeidae	*Caerulea*	Little Blue Heron
Ardeidae	*Thula*	Snowy Egret
Ardeidae	*Tricolor*	Tricoloured Heron
Tyrannidae	*Albiceps*	White-crested Elaenia
Tyrannidae	*Chiriquensis*	Lesser Elaenia
Tyrannidae	*Cristata*	Plain-crested Elaenia
Tyrannidae	*Flavogaster*	Yellow-bellied Elaenia
Tyrannidae	*Mesoleuca*	Olivaceous Elaenia
Tyrannidae	*Obscura*	Highland Elaenia
Tyrannidae	*Pallatangae*	Sierran Elaenia
Tyrannidae	*Parvirostris*	Small-billed Elaenia
Tyrannidae	*Ruficeps*	Rufous-crowned Elaenia
Tyrannidae	*Spectabilis*	Large Elaenia
Accipitridae	*Leucurus*	White-tailed Kite
Momotidae	*Platyrhynchum*	Broad-billed Motmot
Rhinocryptidae	*Indigoticus*	White-breasted Tapaculo
Rhinocryptidae	*Psychopompus*	Chestnut-sided Tapaculo
Caprimulgidae	*Anomalus*	Sickle-winged Nightjar
Caprimulgidae	*Candicans*	White-winged Nightjar
Emberizidae	*Herbicola*	Wedge-tailed Grass-finch
Emberizidae	*Ypiranganus*	Grey-cheeked Grass-finch
Emberizidae	*Longicauda*	Pale-throated Pampa-finch
Emberizidae	*Platensis*	Great Pampa-finch
Tyrannidae	*Alnorum*	Alder Flycatcher
Tyrannidae	*Varius*	Variegated Flycatcher
Thamnophilidae	*Erythrura*	Rufous-tailed Antwren
Thamnophilidae	*Haematonota*	Stipple-throated Antwren
Thamnophilidae	*Leucophthalma*	White-eyed Antwren
Thamnophilidae	*Ornata*	Ornate Antwren
Ramphastidae	*Richardsoni*	Lemon-throated Barbet
Ramphastidae	*Tucinkae*	Scarlet-hooded Barbet
Thraupidae	*Penicillata*	Grey-headed Tanager
Threskiornithidae	*Ruber*	Scarlet Ibis
Trochilidae	*Macroura*	Swallow-tailed Hummingbird
Thraupidae	*Chrysopasta*	White-lored Euphonia
Thraupidae	*Cyanocephala*	Golden-rumped Euphonia
Thraupidae	*Finschi*	Finsch's Euphonia
Thraupidae	*Laniirostris*	Thick-billed Euphonia
Thraupidae	*Minuta*	White-vented Euphonia

Family	Species	Common names (Eng)
Thraupidae	*Pectoralis*	Chestnut-bellied Euphonia
Eurypygidae	*Helias*	Sunbittern
Falconidae	*Columbarius*	Merlin
Falconidae	*Deiroleucus*	Orange-breasted Falcon
Falconidae	*Femoralis*	Aplomado Falcon
Falconidae	*Peregrinus*	Peregrine Falcon, Peregrine
Falconidae	*Rufigularis*	Bat Falcon
Falconidae	*Sparverius*	American Kestrel
Trochilidae	*Fusca*	Black Jacobin
Trochilidae	*Mellivora*	White-necked Jacobin
Formicariidae	*Analis*	Black-faced Antthrush
Formicariidae	*Colma*	Rufous-capped Antthrush
Formicariidae	*Rufifrons*	Rufous-fronted Antthrush
Thamnophilidae	*Erythronotos*	Black-hooded Antwren
Thamnophilidae	*Grisea*	White-fringed Antwren
Thamnophilidae	*Iheringi*	Narrow-billed Antwren
Thamnophilidae	*Littoralis*	Restinga Antwren
Thamnophilidae	*Melanogaster*	Black-bellied Antwren
Thamnophilidae	*Rufa*	Rusty-backed Antwren
Thamnophilidae	*Serrana*	Serra Antwren
Psittacidae	*Modestus*	Dusky-billed Parrotlet
Psittacidae	*Passerinus*	Green-rumped Parrotlet
Psittacidae	*Xanthopterygius*	Blue-winged Parrotlet
Thamnophilidae	*Unduligera*	Undulated Antshrike
Thamnophilidae	*Viridis*	Black-throated Antshrike
Fregatidae	*Ariel*	Lesser Frigatebird
Fregatidae	*Magnificens*	Magnificent Frigatebird
Fregatidae	*Minor*	Greater Frigatebird
Hydrobatidae	*Grallaria*	White-bellied Storm-petrel
Hydrobatidae	*Tropica*	Black-bellied Storm-petrel
Rallidae	*Armillata*	Red-gartered Coot
Rallidae	*Leucoptera*	White-winged Coot
Rallidae	*Rufifrons*	Red-fronted Coot
Furnariidae	*Figulus*	Wing-banded Hornero
Furnariidae	*Leucopus*	Pale-legged Hornero
Furnariidae	*Minor*	Lesser Hornero
Furnariidae	*Rufus*	Rufous Hornero
Furnariidae	*Torridus*	Pale-billed Hornero
Galbulidae	*Purusianus*	Chestnut Jacamar
Galbulidae	*Albirostris*	Yellow-billed Jacamar

Family	Species	Common names (Eng)
Galbulidae	*Chalcothorax*	Purplish Jacamar
Galbulidae	*Cyanescens*	Bluish-fronted Jacamar
Galbulidae	*Cyanicollis*	Blue-necked Jacamar
Galbulidae	*Dea*	Paradise Jacamar
Galbulidae	*Galbula*	Green-tailed Jacamar
Galbulidae	*Leucogastra*	Bronzy Jacamar
Scolopacidae	*Paraguaiae*	South American Snipe
Scolopacidae	*Undulata*	Giant Snipe
Rallidae	*Chloropus*	Common Moorhen
Rallidae	*Melanops*	Spot-flanked Gallinule
Accipitridae	*Swainsonii*	Pearl Kite
Furnariidae	*Cunicularia*	Common Miner
Furnariidae	*Poeciloptera*	Campo Miner
Parulidae	*Aequinoctialis*	Masked Yellowthroat
Columbidae	*Montana*	Ruddy Quail-dove
Columbidae	*Saphirina*	Sapphire Quail-dove
Columbidae	*Violacea*	Violaceous Quail-dove
Accipitridae	*Melanoleucus*	Black-chested Buzzard-eagle
Accipitridae	*Caerulescens*	Crane Hawk
Strigidae	*Minutissimum*	Brazilian Pygmy-owl,
Strigidae	*Mooreorum*	Pernambuco Pygmy-owl
Trochilidae	*Dohrnii*	Hook-billed Hermit
Trochilidae	*Hirsutus*	Rufous-breasted Hermit
Dendrocolaptidae	*Spirurus*	Wedge-billed Woodcreeper
Icteridae	*Chopi*	Chopi Blackbird
Formicariidae	*Eludens*	Elusive Antpitta
Formicariidae	*Guatimalensis*	Scaled Antpitta
Formicariidae	*Varia*	Variegated Antpitta
Parulidae	*Pelzelni*	Rose-breasted Chat
Psittacidae	*Brachyurus*	Short-tailed Parrot
Psittacidae	*Guarouba*	Golden Parakeet
Emberizidae	*Cristata*	Yellow Cardinal
Tyrannidae	*Yetapa*	Streamer-tailed Tyrant
Cuculidae	*Guira*	Guira Cuckoo
Furnariidae	*Hellmayri*	Red-shouldered Spinetail
Laridae	*Alba*	Common White Tern
Cotingidae	*Foetidus*	Bare-necked Fruitcrow
Icteridae	*Mexicanus*	Oriole Blackbird
Cotingidae	*Militaris*	Crimson Fruitcrow
Procellariidae	*Caerulea*	Blue Petrel

Family	Species	Common names (Eng)
Emberizidae	*Unicolor*	Uniform Finch
Accipitridae	*Bidentatus*	Double-toothed Kite
Accipitridae	*Diodon*	Rufous-thighed Kite
Accipitridae	*Harpyja*	Harpy Eagle
Accipitridae	*Coronatus*	Crowned Eagle
Trochilidae	*Bilophus*	Horned Sungem
Accipitridae	*Hamatus*	Slender-billed Kite
Furnariidae	*Contaminatus*	Sharp-billed Treehunter
Trochilidae	*Aurescens*	Gould's Jewelfront
Trochilidae	*Schreibersii*	Black-throated Brilliant
Trochilidae	*Xanthogonys*	Velvet-browed Brilliant
Trochilidae	*Furcifer*	Blue-tufted Starthroat
Trochilidae	*Longirostris*	Long-billed Starthroat
Trochilidae	*Squamosus*	Stripe-breasted Starthroat
Heliornithidae	*Fulica*	Sungrebe
Trochilidae	*Auritus*	Black-eared Fairy
Thraupidae	*Flavicollis*	Yellow-backed Tanager
Thraupidae	*Guira*	Guira Tanager
Thraupidae	*Ruficapilla*	Rufous-headed Tanager
Tyrannidae	*Iohannis*	Johannes's Tody-tyrant
Tyrannidae	*Josephinae*	Boat-billed Tody-tyrant
Tyrannidae	*Kaempferi*	Kaempfer's Tody-tyrant
Tyrannidae	*Nidipendulus*	Hangnest Tody-tyrant
Tyrannidae	*Obsoletus*	Brown-breasted Bamboo-tyrant
Tyrannidae	*Orbitatus*	Eye-ringed Tody-tyrant
Troglodytidae	*Leucosticta*	White-breasted Wood-wren
Falconidae	*Cachinnans*	Laughing Falcon
Thamnophilidae	*Atricapillus*	Black-capped Antwren
Thamnophilidae	*Dorsimaculatus*	Spot-backed Antwren
Thamnophilidae	*Longirostris*	Large-billed Antwren
Thamnophilidae	*Pectoralis*	Pectoral Antwren
Thamnophilidae	*Sellowi*	Caatinga Antwren
Thamnophilidae	*Stictocephalus*	Todd's Antwren
Thamnophilidae	*Sticturus*	Spot-tailed Antwren
Pipridae	*Flavivertex*	Yellow-crested Manakin
Pipridae	*Linteatus*	Flame-crested Manakin
Anatidae	*Atricapilla*	Black-headed Duck
Recurvirostridae	*Mexicanus*	Black-necked Stilt
Tyrannidae	*Ferruginea*	Cliff Flycatcher
Hirundinidae	*Rustica*	Barn Swallow

Family	Species	Common names (Eng)
Caprimulgidae	*Climacocerca*	Ladder-tailed Nightjar
Caprimulgidae	*Torquata*	Scissor-tailed Nightjar
Dendrocolaptidae	*Brigidai*	Mato Grosso Woodcreeper
Dendrocolaptidae	*Perrotii*	Red-billed Woodcreeper
Dendrocolaptidae	*Stresemanni*	Bar-bellied Woodcreeper
Dendrocolaptidae	*Uniformis*	Uniform Woodcreeper
Trochilidae	*Chrysura*	Gilded Hummingbird
Trochilidae	*Cyanus*	White-chinned Sapphire
Trochilidae	*Sapphirina*	Rufous-throated Sapphire
Furnariidae	*Rectirostris*	Chestnut-capped Foliage-gleaner
Furnariidae	*Subulatus*	Striped Woodhaunter
Formicariidae	*Berlepschi*	Amazonian Antpitta
Formicariidae	*Macularius*	Spotted Antpitta
Formicariidae	*Nattereri*	Speckle-breasted Antpitta
Formicariidae	*Ochroleucus*	White-browed Antpitta
Vireonidae	*Amaurocephalus*	Grey-eyed Greenlet
Vireonidae	*Brunneiceps*	Brown-headed Greenlet
Vireonidae	*Hypoxanthus*	Dusky-capped Greenlet
Vireonidae	*Pectoralis*	Ashy-headed Greenlet
Vireonidae	*Poicilotis*	Rufous-crowned Greenlet
Vireonidae	*Sclateri*	Tepuí Greenlet
Vireonidae	*Semicinereus*	Grey-chested Greenlet
Vireonidae	*Thoracicus*	Lemon-chested Greenlet
Thamnophilidae	*Naevius*	Spot-backed Antbird
Thamnophilidae	*Punctulatus*	Dot-backed Antbird
Tyrannidae	*Perspicillatus*	Spectacled Tyrant
Thamnophilidae	*Cantator*	Guianan Warbling-antbird
Thamnophilidae	*Flavescens*	Imeri Warbling-antbird
Thamnophilidae	*Hypoxantha*	Yellow-browed Antbird
Thamnophilidae	*Ochrogyna*	Rondonia Warbling-antbird
Thamnophilidae	*Peruviana*	Peruvian Warbling-antbird
Thamnophilidae	*Striata*	Spix's Warbling-antbird
Thamnophilidae	*Subflava*	Yellow-breasted Warbling-antbird
Thamnophilidae	*Guttatus*	Spot-backed Antshrike
Falconidae	*Americanus*	Red-throated Caracara
Icteridae	*Cayanensis*	Epaulet Oriole
Icteridae	*Croconotus*	Orange-backed Troupial
Icteridae	*Jamacaii*	Campo Troupial
Icteridae	*Nigrogularis*	Yellow Oriole
Accipitridae	*Mississippiensis*	Mississippi Kite

Family	Species	Common names (Eng)
Accipitridae	*Plumbea*	Plumbeous Kite
Pipridae	*Militaris*	Pin-tailed Manakin
Tyrannidae	*Caudata*	Pale-tipped Tyrannulet
Tyrannidae	*Inornata*	Plain Tyrannulet
Tyrannidae	*Subflava*	Amazonian Inezia
Cotingidae	*Fusca*	Dusky Purpletuft
Cotingidae	*Isabellae*	White-browed Purpletuft
Cotingidae	*Pipra*	Buff-throated Purpletuft
Ardeidae	*Exilis*	Least Bittern
Ardeidae	*Involucris*	Stripe-backed Bittern
Ciconiidae	*Mycteria*	Jabiru
Galbulidae	*Tridactyla*	Three-toed Jacamar
Galbulidae	*Aureus*	Great Jacamar
Jacanidae	*Jacana*	Wattled Jacana
Trochilidae	*Guimeti*	Violet-headed Hummingbird
Tyrannidae	*Striaticeps*	Cinereous Tyrant
Icteridae	*Tanagrinus*	Velvet-fronted Grackle
Thraupidae	*Melanoleuca*	Red-billed Pied Tanager
Cotingidae	*Elegans*	Brazilian Laniisoma
Thraupidae	*Fulvus*	Fulvous Shrike-tanager
Thraupidae	*Versicolor*	White-winged Shrike-tanager
Cotingidae	*Hypopyrra*	Cinereous Mourner
Laridae	*Atlanticus*	Olrog's Gull
Laridae	*Atricilla*	Laughing Gull
Laridae	*Cirrocephalus*	Grey-headed Gull
Laridae	*Delawarensis*	Ring-billed Gull
Laridae	*Dominicanus*	Kelp Gull
Laridae	*Maculipennis*	Brown-hooded Gull
Laridae	*Pipixcan*	Franklin's Gull
Rallidae	*Exilis*	Grey-breasted Crake
Rallidae	*Jamaicensis*	Black Rail
Rallidae	*Leucopyrrhus*	Red-and-white Crake
Rallidae	*Melanophaius*	Rufous-sided Crake
Rallidae	*Xenopterus*	Rufous-faced Crake
Tyrannidae	*Euleri*	Euler's Flycatcher
Tyrannidae	*Leucophaius*	Piratic Flycatcher
Dendrocolaptidae	*Albolineatus*	Lineated Woodcreeper
Dendrocolaptidae	*Angustirostris*	Narrow-billed Woodcreeper
Dendrocolaptidae	*Falcinellus*	Scalloped Woodcreeper
Dendrocolaptidae	*Souleyetii*	Streak-headed Woodcreeper

Family	Species	Common names (Eng)
Dendrocolaptidae	*Squamatus*	Scaled Woodcreeper
Pipridae	*Coronata*	Blue-crowned Manakin
Pipridae	*Iris*	Opal-crowned Manakin
Pipridae	*Nattereri*	Snow-capped Manakin
Pipridae	*Serena*	White-fronted Manakin
Pipridae	*Suavissima*	Orange-bellied Manakin
Pipridae	*Vilasboasi*	Golden-crowned Manakin
Furnariidae	*Platensis*	Tufted Tit-spinetail
Furnariidae	*Setaria*	Araucaria Tit-spinetail
Furnariidae	*Striolata*	Striolated Tit-spinetail
Accipitridae	*Cayanensis*	Grey-headed Kite
Accipitridae	*Forbesi*	White-collared Kite
Tyrannidae	*Amaurocephalus*	Sepia-capped Flycatcher
Tyrannidae	*Superciliaris*	Slaty-capped Flycatcher
Columbidae	*Rufaxilla*	Grey-fronted Dove
Columbidae	*Verreauxi*	White-tipped Dove
Trochilidae	*Chlorocercus*	Olive-spotted Hummingbird
Trochilidae	*Albicollis*	White-throated Hummingbird
Accipitridae	*Albicollis*	White Hawk
Accipitridae	*Kuhli*	White-browed Hawk
Accipitridae	*Lacernulatus*	White-necked Hawk
Accipitridae	*Melanops*	Black-faced Hawk
Accipitridae	*Polionotus*	Mantled Hawk
Accipitridae	*Schistaceus*	Slate-coloured Hawk
Furnariidae	*Rectirostris*	Straight-billed Reedhaunter
Scolopacidae	*Griseus*	Short-billed Dowitcher
Furnariidae	*Curvirostris*	Curve-billed Reedhaunter
Scolopacidae	*Haemastica*	Hudsonian Godwit
Rhinocryptidae	*Thoracicus*	Rusty-belted Tapaculo
Cotingidae	*Lanioides*	Cinnamon-vented Piha
Cotingidae	*Streptophorus*	Rose-collared Piha
Cotingidae	*Vociferans*	Screaming Piha
Furnariidae	*Nematura*	Sharp-tailed Streamcreeper
Trochilidae	*Chalybeus*	Festive Coquette
Trochilidae	*Gouldii*	Dot-eared Coquette
Trochilidae	*Magnificus*	Frilled Coquette
Trochilidae	*Ornatus*	Tufted Coquette
Trochilidae	*Pavoninus*	Peacock Coquette
Strigidae	*Cristata*	Crested Owl
Tyrannidae	*Eulophotes*	Long-crested Pygmy-tyrant

Family	Species	Common names (Eng)
Tyrannidae	*Galeatus*	Helmeted Pygmy-tyrant
Caprimulgidae	*Semitorquatus*	Short-tailed Nighthawk
Pipridae	*Pyrocephalus*	Fiery-capped Manakin
Pipridae	*Regulus*	Striped Manakin
Tyrannidae	*Rixosa*	Cattle Tyrant
Thamnophilidae	*Leachii*	Large-tailed Antshrike
Thamnophilidae	*Severa*	Tufted Antshrike
Icteridae	*Imthurni*	Golden-tufted Grackle
Procellariidae	*Giganteus*	Southern Giant-petrel
Procellariidae	*Halli*	Northern Giant-petrel
Caprimulgidae	*Forcipata*	Long-trained Nightjar
Bucconidae	*Fusca*	White-chested Puffbird
Bucconidae	*Rufa*	Rufous-necked Puffbird
Bucconidae	*Semicincta*	Semicollared Puffbird
Bucconidae	*Striata*	Crescent-chested Puffbird
Pipridae	*Manacus*	White-bearded Manakin
Tyrannidae	*Leucophrys*	White-throated Tyrannulet
Alcedinidae	*Torquata*	Ringed Kingfisher
Tyrannidae	*Pitangua*	Boat-billed Flycatcher
Strigidae	*Atricapilla*	Black-capped Screech-owl
Strigidae	*Choliba*	Tropical Screech-owl
Strigidae	*Guatemalae*	Vermiculated Screech-owl
Strigidae	*Sanctaecatarinae*	Long-tufted Screech-owl
Strigidae	*Watsonii*	Tawny-bellied Screech-owl
Thamnophilidae	*Margaritatus*	Pearly Antshrike
Furnariidae	*Parnaguae*	Great Xenops
Picidae	*Cactorum*	White-fronted Woodpecker
Picidae	*Candidus*	White Woodpecker
Picidae	*Cruentatus*	Yellow-tufted Woodpecker
Picidae	*Flavifrons*	Yellow-fronted Woodpecker
Rhinocryptidae	*Torquata*	Collared Crescentchest
Anatidae	*Octosetaceus*	Brazilian Merganser
Rhinocryptidae	*Ater*	Slaty Bristlefront
Rhinocryptidae	*Stresemanni*	Stresemann's Bristlefront
Threskiornithidae	*Cayennensis*	Green Ibis
Furnariidae	*Aurantiaca*	Orange-fronted Plushcrown
Falconidae	*Buckleyi*	Buckley's Forest-falcon
Falconidae	*Gilvicollis*	Lined Forest-falcon
Falconidae	*Mintoni*	Cryptic Forest-falcon
Falconidae	*Mirandollei*	Slaty-backed Forest-falcon

Family	Species	Common names (Eng)
Falconidae	*Ruficollis*	Barred Forest-falcon
Falconidae	*Semitorquatus*	Collared Forest-falcon
Polioptilidae	*Collaris*	Collared Gnatwren
Troglodytidae	*Bambla*	Wing-banded Wren
Troglodytidae	*Marginatus*	Scaly-breasted Wren
Troglodytidae	*Ustulatus*	Flutist Wren
Bucconidae	*Lanceolata*	Lanceolated Monklet
Rallidae	*Schomburgkii*	Ocellated Crake
Thamnophilidae	*Quixensis*	Dot-winged Antwren
Falconidae	*Chimachima*	Yellow-headed Caracara
Falconidae	*Chimango*	Chimango Caracara
Mimidae	*Gilvus*	Tropical Mockingbird
Mimidae	*Saturninus*	Chalk-browed Mockingbird
Mimidae	*Triurus*	White-banded Mockingbird
Tyrannidae	*Macconnelli*	Macconnell's Flycatcher
Tyrannidae	*Oleagineus*	Ochre-bellied Flycatcher
Tyrannidae	*Rufiventris*	Grey-hooded Flycatcher
Thraupidae	*Oleagineus*	Olive-backed Tanager
Cracidae	*Mitu*	Alagoas Curassow
Cracidae	*Tomentosum*	Crestless Curassow
Cracidae	*Tuberosum*	Razor-billed Curassow
Icteridae	*Bonariensis*	Shiny Cowbird
Icteridae	*Oryzivorus*	Giant Cowbird
Icteridae	*Rufoaxillaris*	Screaming Cowbird
Momotidae	*Momota*	Blue-crowned Motmot
Bucconidae	*Atra*	Black Nunbird
Bucconidae	*Flavirostris*	Yellow-billed Nunbird
Bucconidae	*Morphoeus*	White-fronted Nunbird
Bucconidae	*Nigrifrons*	Black-fronted Nunbird
Accipitridae	*Guianensis*	Crested Eagle, Guianan Crested Eagle
Tyrannidae	*Vetula*	Shear-tailed Grey-tyrant
Ciconiidae	*Americana*	Wood Stork
Tyrannidae	*Ferox*	Short-crested Flycatcher
Tyrannidae	*Swainsoni*	Swainson's Flycatcher
Tyrannidae	*Tuberculifer*	Dusky-capped Flycatcher
Tyrannidae	*Tyrannulus*	Brown-crested Flycatcher
Tyrannidae	*Atricaudus*	Black-tailed Flycatcher
Tyrannidae	*Barbatus*	Bearded Flycatcher
Parulidae	*Castaneocapilla*	Tepui Redstart
Parulidae	*Miniatus*	Slate-throated Redstart

Family	Species	Common names (Eng)
Tyrannidae	*Luteiventris*	Sulphur-bellied Flycatcher
Tyrannidae	*Maculatus*	Streaked Flycatcher
Tyrannidae	*Caniceps*	Grey Elaenia
Tyrannidae	*Flavivertex*	Yellow-crowned Elaenia
Tyrannidae	*Gaimardii*	Forest Elaenia
Tyrannidae	*Viridicata*	Greenish Elaenia
Psittacidae	*Monachus*	Monk Parakeet
Tyrannidae	*Cayanensis*	Rusty-margined Flycatcher
Tyrannidae	*Granadensis*	Grey-capped Flycatcher
Tyrannidae	*Luteiventris*	Dusky-chested Flycatcher
Tyrannidae	*Similis*	Social Flycatcher
Thamnophilidae	*Atrothorax*	Black-throated Antbird
Thamnophilidae	*Disjuncta*	Yapacana Antbird
Thamnophilidae	*Ferruginea*	Ferruginous-backed Antbird
Thamnophilidae	*Fortis*	Sooty Antbird
Thamnophilidae	*Goeldii*	Goeldi's Antbird
Thamnophilidae	*Hemimelaena*	Chestnut-tailed Antbird
Thamnophilidae	*Hyperythra*	Plumbeous Antbird
Thamnophilidae	*Longipes*	White-bellied Antbird
Thamnophilidae	*Loricata*	White-bibbed Antbird
Thamnophilidae	*Melanoceps*	White-shouldered Antbird
Thamnophilidae	*Pelzelni*	Grey-bellied Antbird
Thamnophilidae	*Ruficauda*	Scalloped Antbird
Thamnophilidae	*Squamosa*	Squamate Antbird
Thamnophilidae	*Leucophrys*	White-browed Antbird
Thamnophilidae	*Lugubris*	Ash-breasted Antbird
Thamnophilidae	*Myotherinus*	Black-faced Antbird
Thamnophilidae	*Hemileucus*	Black-and-white Antbird
Thamnophilidae	*Strigilatus*	Stripe-backed Antbird
Thamnophilidae	*Torquata*	Wing-banded Antbird
Formicariidae	*Campanisona*	Thrush-like Antpitta
Formicariidae	*Simplex*	Brown-breasted Antpitta
Thamnophilidae	*Ambigua*	Yellow-throated Antwren
Thamnophilidae	*Assimilis*	Leaden Antwren
Thamnophilidae	*Axillaris*	White-flanked Antwren
Thamnophilidae	*Behni*	Plain-winged Antwren
Thamnophilidae	*Brachyura*	Pygmy Antwren
Thamnophilidae	*Cherriei*	Cherrie's Antwren
Thamnophilidae	*Fluminensis*	Rio De Janeiro Antwren
Thamnophilidae	*Gularis*	Star-throated Antwren

Family	Species	Common names (Eng)
Thamnophilidae	*Guttata*	Rufous-bellied Antwren
Thamnophilidae	*Gutturalis*	Brown-bellied Antwren
Thamnophilidae	*Hauxwelli*	Plain-throated Antwren
Thamnophilidae	*Ignota*	Moustached Antwren
Thamnophilidae	*Iheringi*	Ihering's Antwren
Thamnophilidae	*Klagesi*	Klages's Antwren
Thamnophilidae	*Longipennis*	Long-winged Antwren
Thamnophilidae	*Menetriesii*	Grey Antwren
Thamnophilidae	*Minor*	Salvadori's Antwren
Thamnophilidae	*Multostriata*	Amazonian Streaked Antwren
Thamnophilidae	*Sclateri*	Sclater's Antwren
Thamnophilidae	*Snowi*	Alagoas Antwren
Thamnophilidae	*Sunensis*	Rio Suno Antwren
Thamnophilidae	*Surinamensis*	Guianan Streaked Antwren
Thamnophilidae	*Unicolor*	Unicoloured Antwren, Unicolored Antwren
Thamnophilidae	*Urosticta*	Band-tailed Antwren
Psittacidae	*Nenday*	Nanday Parakeet
Psittacidae	*Panychlora*	Tepui Parrotlet
Dendrocolaptidae	*Longirostris*	Long-billed Woodcreeper
Thraupidae	*Pileata*	Hooded Tanager
Thraupidae	*Rourei*	Cherry-throated Tanager
Hirundinidae	*Tibialis*	White-thighed Swallow
Anatidae	*Jubata*	Orinoco Goose
Rallidae	*Erythrops*	Paint-billed Crake
Thamnophilidae	*Niger*	Black Bushbird
Cuculidae	*Geoffroyi*	Rufous-vented Ground-cuckoo
Cuculidae	*Pucheranii*	Red-billed Ground-cuckoo
Cuculidae	*Rufipennis*	Rufous-winged Ground-cuckoo
Cuculidae	*Squamiger*	Scaled Ground-cuckoo
Pipridae	*Aurifrons*	Wied's Tyrant-manakin
Thraupidae	*Fasciata*	White-banded Tanager
Anatidae	*Peposaca*	Rosy-billed Pochard
Anatidae	*Dominicus*	Masked Duck
Bucconidae	*Amaurocephala*	Chestnut-headed Nunlet
Bucconidae	*Rubecula*	Rusty-breasted Nunlet
Bucconidae	*Ruficapilla*	Rufous-capped Nunlet
Bucconidae	*Sclateri*	Fulvous-chinned Nunlet
Bucconidae	*Hyperrhynchus*	White-necked Puffbird
Bucconidae	*Macrorhynchos*	Guianan Puffbird
Bucconidae	*Ordii*	Brown-banded Puffbird

BIRDS		Kingdom: Animalia
Family	*Species*	**Common names (Eng)**
Bucconidae	*Swainsoni*	Buff-bellied Puffbird
Bucconidae	*Tectus*	Pied Puffbird
Cracidae	*Urumutum*	Nocturnal Curassow
Tinamidae	*Boraquira*	White-bellied Nothura
Tinamidae	*Maculosa*	Spotted Nothura
Tinamidae	*Minor*	Lesser Nothura
Scolopacidae	*Borealis*	Eskimo Curlew
Scolopacidae	*Phaeopus*	Whimbrel
Ardeidae	*Violacea*	Yellow-crowned Night-heron
Nyctibiidae	*Aethereus*	Long-tailed Potoo
Nyctibiidae	*Bracteatus*	Rufous Potoo
Nyctibiidae	*Grandis*	Great Potoo
Nyctibiidae	*Griseus*	Grey Potoo
Nyctibiidae	*Leucopterus*	White-winged Potoo
Ardeidae	*Nycticorax*	Black-crowned Night-heron
Caprimulgidae	*Albicollis*	Common Pauraque
Caprimulgidae	*Ocellatus*	Ocellated Poorwill
Caprimulgidae	*Leucopyga*	Band-tailed Nighthawk
Caprimulgidae	*Vielliardi*	Plain-tailed Nighthawk
Bucconidae	*Chacuru*	White-eared Puffbird
Bucconidae	*Maculatus*	Spot-backed Puffbird
Bucconidae	*Striolatus*	Striolated Puffbird
Hydrobatidae	*Oceanicus*	Wilson's Storm-petrel
Hydrobatidae	*Leucorhoa*	Leach's Storm-petrel
Icteridae	*Latirostris*	Band-tailed Oropendola
Odontophoridae	*Capueira*	Spot-winged Wood-quail
Odontophoridae	*Gujanensis*	Marbled Wood-quail
Troglodytidae	*Cinereus*	Tooth-billed Wren
Tyrannidae	*Coronatus*	Amazonian Royal Flycatcher
Opisthocomidae	*Hoazin*	Hoatzin
Parulidae	*Agilis*	Connecticut Warbler
Thraupidae	*Abeillei*	Brown Tanager
Charadriidae	*Ruficollis*	Tawny-throated Dotterel
Furnariidae	*Moreirae*	Itatiaia Thistletail
Tyrannidae	*Inerme*	White-lored Tyrannulet
Cracidae	*Canicollis*	Chaco Chachalaca
Cracidae	*Guttata*	Speckled Chachalaca
Thraupidae	*Chloricterus*	Olive-green Tanager
Psittacidae	*Manilata*	Red-bellied Macaw
Emberizidae	*Angolensis*	Lesser Seed-finch

Family	Species	Common names (Eng)
Emberizidae	*Crassirostris*	Large-billed Seed-finch
Emberizidae	*Maximiliani*	Great-billed Seed-finch
Cotingidae	*Cristatus*	Sharpbill
Anatidae	*Vittata*	Lake Duck
Procellariidae	*Belcheri*	Thin-billed Prion
Procellariidae	*Desolata*	Antarctic Prion
Cotingidae	*Castaneus*	Chestnut-crowned Becard
Cotingidae	*Marginatus*	Black-capped Becard
Cotingidae	*Minor*	Pink-throated Becard
Cotingidae	*Polychopterus*	White-winged Becard
Cotingidae	*Rufus*	Cinereous Becard
Accipitridae	*Haliaetus*	Osprey
Apodidae	*Cayennensis*	Lesser Swallow-tailed Swift
Accipitridae	*Unicinctus*	Harris's Hawk
Rallidae	*Maculatus*	Spotted Rail
Rallidae	*Nigricans*	Blackish Rail
Rallidae	*Sanguinolentus*	Plumbeous Rail
Cardinalidae	*Humeralis*	Yellow-shouldered Grosbeak
Emberizidae	*Baeri*	Crimson-fronted Cardinal
Emberizidae	*Capitata*	Yellow-billed Cardinal
Emberizidae	*Coronata*	Red-crested Cardinal
Parulidae	*Pitiayumi*	Tropical Parula
Passeridae	*Domesticus*	House Sparrow
Columbidae	*Cayennensis*	Pale-vented Pigeon
Columbidae	*Fasciata*	Band-tailed Pigeon
Columbidae	*Maculosa*	Spot-winged Pigeon
Columbidae	*Picazuro*	Picazuro Pigeon
Columbidae	*Plumbea*	Plumbeous Pigeon
Columbidae	*Speciosa*	Scaled Pigeon
Columbidae	*Subvinacea*	Ruddy Pigeon
Pelecanidae	*Occidentalis*	Brown Pelican
Cracidae	*Jacquacu*	Spix's Guan
Cracidae	*Jacucaca*	White-browed Guan
Cracidae	*Marail*	Marail Guan
Cracidae	*Obscura*	Dusky-legged Guan
Cracidae	*Ochrogaster*	Chestnut-bellied Guan
Cracidae	*Pileata*	White-crested Guan
Cracidae	*Superciliaris*	Rusty-margined Guan
Thamnophilidae	*Lophotes*	White-lined Antbird
Thamnophilidae	*Rufifrons*	Black-headed Antbird

Family	Species	Common names (Eng)
Cardinalidae	*Erythromelas*	Red-and-black Grosbeak
Cotingidae	*Tricolor*	Capuchinbird
Hirundinidae	*Pyrrhonota*	Cliff Swallow, American Cliff Swallow
Furnariidae	*Erythrophthalmus*	Red-eyed Thornbird
Furnariidae	*Ferrugineigula*	Orange-eyed Thornbird
Furnariidae	*Ruber*	Greater Thornbird
Furnariidae	*Rufifrons*	Rufous-fronted Thornbird
Furnariidae	*Striaticollis*	Freckle-breasted Thornbird
Parulidae	*Fulvicauda*	Buff-rumped Warbler
Parulidae	*Rivularis*	Riverbank Warbler
Phaethontidae	*Aethereus*	Red-billed Tropicbird
Phaethontidae	*Lepturus*	White-tailed Tropicbird
Trochilidae	*Augusti*	Sooty-capped Hermit
Trochilidae	*Bourcieri*	Straight-billed Hermit
Trochilidae	*Eurynome*	Scale-throated Hermit
Trochilidae	*Griseogularis*	Grey-chinned Hermit
Trochilidae	*Hispidus*	White-bearded Hermit
Trochilidae	*Idaliae*	Minute Hermit
Trochilidae	*Longuemareus*	Little Hermit
Trochilidae	*Malaris*	Great-billed Hermit
Trochilidae	*Nattereri*	Cinnamon-throated Hermit
Trochilidae	*Philippii*	Needle-billed Hermit
Trochilidae	*Pretrei*	Planalto Hermit
Trochilidae	*Ruber*	Reddish Hermit
Trochilidae	*Rupurumii*	Streak-throated Hermit
Laridae	*Simplex*	Large-billed Tern
Phalacrocoracidae	*Brasilianus*	Neotropic Cormorant
Trogonidae	*Pavoninus*	Pavonine Quetzal
Cardinalidae	*Aureoventris*	Black-backed Grosbeak
Cotingidae	*Flavirostris*	Swallow-tailed Cotinga
Furnariidae	*Atricapillus*	Black-capped Foliage-gleaner
Furnariidae	*Erythrocercum*	Rufous-rumped Foliage-gleaner
Furnariidae	*Erythropterum*	Chestnut-winged Foliage-gleaner
Furnariidae	*Lichtensteini*	Ochre-breasted Foliage-gleaner
Furnariidae	*Rufum*	Buff-fronted Foliage-gleaner
Threskiornithidae	*Infuscatus*	Bare-faced Ibis, Whispering Ibis
Thamnophilidae	*Erythroptera*	Reddish-winged Bare-eye
Thamnophilidae	*Nigromaculata*	Black-spotted Bare-eye
Furnariidae	*Melanops*	Wren-like Rushbird
Cotingidae	*Rutila*	White-tipped Plantcutter

Family	Species	Common names (Eng)
Cuculidae	*Cayana*	Squirrel Cuckoo
Cuculidae	*Melanogaster*	Black-bellied Cuckoo
Picidae	*Aurulentus*	White-browed Woodpecker
Picidae	*Chrysochloros*	Golden-green Woodpecker
Picidae	*Flavigula*	Yellow-throated Woodpecker
Picidae	*Leucolaemus*	White-throated Woodpecker
Picidae	*Albosquamatus*	White-wedged Piculet
Picidae	*Aurifrons*	Bar-breasted Piculet
Picidae	*Castelnau*	Plain-breasted Piculet
Picidae	*Cirratus*	White-barred Piculet
Picidae	*Exilis*	Golden-spangled Piculet
Picidae	*Fulvescens*	Tawny Piculet
Picidae	*Fuscus*	Rusty-necked Piculet
Picidae	*Lafresnayi*	Lafresnaye's Piculet
Picidae	*Limae*	Ochraceous Piculet
Picidae	*Nebulosus*	Mottled Piculet
Picidae	*Pumilus*	Orinoco Piculet
Picidae	*Pygmaeus*	Spotted Piculet
Picidae	*Rufiventris*	Rufous-breasted Piculet
Picidae	*Spilogaster*	White-bellied Piculet
Picidae	*Temminckii*	Ochre-collared Piculet
Picidae	*Varzeae*	Varzea Piculet
Ardeidae	*Pileatus*	Capped Heron
Psittacidae	*Leucogaster*	White-bellied Parrot
Psittacidae	*Melanocephalus*	Black-headed Parrot
Psittacidae	*Pileata*	Pileated Parrot, Red-capped Parrot
Psittacidae	*Fuscus*	Dusky Parrot
Psittacidae	*Maximiliani*	Scaly-headed Parrot
Psittacidae	*Menstruus*	Blue-headed Parrot
Cracidae	*Cujubi*	Red-throated Piping-guan
Cracidae	*Cumanensis*	Blue-throated Piping-guan
Cracidae	*Jacutinga*	Black-fronted Piping-guan
Pipridae	*Aureola*	Crimson-hooded Manakin
Pipridae	*Chloromeros*	Round-tailed Manakin
Pipridae	*Cornuta*	Scarlet-horned Manakin
Pipridae	*Erythrocephala*	Golden-headed Manakin
Pipridae	*Fasciicauda*	Band-tailed Manakin
Pipridae	*Filicauda*	Wire-tailed Manakin
Pipridae	*Pipra*	White-crowned Manakin
Pipridae	*Rubrocapilla*	Red-headed Manakin

Family	Species	Common names (Eng)
Thraupidae	*Melanonota*	Fawn-breasted Tanager
Pipridae	*Chloris*	Wing-barred Piprites
Pipridae	*Pileata*	Black-capped Piprites
Thraupidae	*Flava*	Hepatic Tanager
Thraupidae	*Leucoptera*	White-winged Tanager
Thraupidae	*Olivacea*	Scarlet Tanager
Thraupidae	*Rubra*	Summer Tanager
Tyrannidae	*Lictor*	Lesser Kiskadee
Tyrannidae	*Sulphuratus*	Great Kiskadee
Thamnophilidae	*Albifrons*	White-plumed Antbird
Threskiornithidae	*Ajaja*	Roseate Spoonbill
Tyrannidae	*Coronatus*	Golden-crowned Spadebill
Tyrannidae	*Leucoryphus*	Russet-winged Spadebill
Tyrannidae	*Mystaceus*	White-throated Spadebill
Tyrannidae	*Platyrhynchos*	White-crested Spadebill
Tyrannidae	*Saturatus*	Cinnamon-crested Spadebill
Threskiornithidae	*Chihi*	White-faced Ibis
Charadriidae	*Squatarola*	Grey Plover, Black-bellied Plover
Podicipedidae	*Major*	Great Grebe
Podicipedidae	*Podiceps*	Pied-billed Grebe
Tyrannidae	*Capitalis*	Black-and-white Tody-flycatcher
Tyrannidae	*Fumifrons*	Smoky-fronted Tody-flycatcher
Tyrannidae	*Latirostris*	Rusty-fronted Tody-flycatcher
Tyrannidae	*Plumbeiceps*	Ochre-faced Tody-flycatcher
Tyrannidae	*Pectoralis*	Bearded Tachuri
Tyrannidae	*Superciliaris*	Grey-backed Tachuri
Trochilidae	*Guainumbi*	White-tailed Goldenthroat
Trochilidae	*Milleri*	Tepui Goldenthroat
Trochilidae	*Theresiae*	Green-tailed Goldenthroat
Emberizidae	*Cinerea*	Cinereous Warbling-finch
Emberizidae	*Lateralis*	Red-rumped Warbling-finch
Emberizidae	*Nigrorufa*	Black-and-rufous Warbling-finch
Emberizidae	*Thoracica*	Bay-chested Warbling-finch
Rallidae	*Flavirostris*	Azure Gallinule
Cotingidae	*Porphyrolaema*	Purple-throated Cotinga
Emberizidae	*Caerulescens*	Blue Finch
Rallidae	*Albicollis*	Ash-throated Crake
Rallidae	*Flaviventer*	Yellow-breasted Crake
Rallidae	*Spiloptera*	Dot-winged Crake
Psittacidae	*Auricollis*	Golden-collared Macaw

Family	Species	Common names (Eng)
Psittacidae	*Couloni*	Blue-headed Macaw
Psittacidae	*Maracana*	Blue-winged Macaw
Procellariidae	*Aequinoctialis*	White-chinned Petrel
Procellariidae	*Conspicillata*	Spectacled Petrel
Cotingidae	*Albus*	White Bellbird
Cotingidae	*Averano*	Bearded Bellbird
Cotingidae	*Nudicollis*	Bare-throated Bellbird
Hirundinidae	*Chalybea*	Grey-breasted Martin
Hirundinidae	*Elegans*	Southern Martin
Hirundinidae	*Subis*	Purple Martin
Hirundinidae	*Tapera*	Brown-chested Martin
Icteridae	*Angustifrons*	Russet-backed Oropendola
Icteridae	*Decumanus*	Crested Oropendola
Icteridae	*Viridis*	Green Oropendola
Tyrannidae	*Flaviventris*	Warbling Doradito
Tyrannidae	*Sclateri*	Crested Doradito
Icteridae	*Guirahuro*	Yellow-rumped Marshbird
Icteridae	*Virescens*	Brown-and-yellow Marshbird
Strigidae	*Clamator*	Striped Owl
Furnariidae	*Cristata*	Caatinga Cacholote
Furnariidae	*Lophotes*	Brown Cacholote
Furnariidae	*Unirufa*	Rufous Cacholote
Rhinocryptidae	*Guttatus*	Spotted Bamboowren
Psophiidae	*Crepitans*	Grey-winged Trumpeter
Psophiidae	*Leucoptera*	Pale-winged Trumpeter
Psophiidae	*Viridis*	Dark-winged Trumpeter
Procellariidae	*Arminjoniana*	Trindade Petrel
Procellariidae	*Incerta*	Atlantic Petrel
Ramphastidae	*Aracari*	Black-necked Aracari
Ramphastidae	*Azara*	Ivory-billed Aracari
Ramphastidae	*Bailloni*	Saffron Toucanet
Ramphastidae	*Beauharnaesii*	Curl-crested Aracari
Ramphastidae	*Bitorquatus*	Red-necked Aracari
Ramphastidae	*Castanotis*	Chestnut-eared Aracari
Ramphastidae	*Inscriptus*	Lettered Aracari
Ramphastidae	*Pluricinctus*	Many-banded Aracari
Ramphastidae	*Viridis*	Green Aracari
Procellariidae	*Griseus*	Sooty Shearwater
Procellariidae	*Puffinus*	Manx Shearwater
Strigidae	*Koeniswaldiana*	Tawny-browed Owl

Family	Species	Common names (Eng)
Strigidae	*Perspicillata*	Spectacled Owl
Thamnophilidae	*Stellaris*	Spot-winged Antshrike
Hirundinidae	*Cyanoleuca*	Blue-and-white Swallow
Thamnophilidae	*Atra*	Fringe-backed Fire-eye
Thamnophilidae	*Leuconota*	White-backed Fire-eye
Thamnophilidae	*Leucoptera*	White-shouldered Fire-eye
Psittacidae	*Aurantiocephala*	Bald Parrot
Psittacidae	*Barrabandi*	Orange-cheeked Parrot
Psittacidae	*Caica*	Caica Parrot
Psittacidae	*Vulturina*	Vulturine Parrot
Tyrannidae	*Rubinus*	Vermilion Flycatcher
Cotingidae	*Scutatus*	Red-ruffed Fruitcrow
Thraupidae	*Ruficeps*	Chestnut-headed Tanager
Psittacidae	*Cruentata*	Blue-throated Parakeet
Psittacidae	*Devillei*	Blaze-winged Parakeet
Psittacidae	*Egregia*	Fiery-shouldered Parakeet
Psittacidae	*Frontalis*	Maroon-bellied Parakeet
Psittacidae	*Griseipectus*	Grey-breasted Parakeet
Psittacidae	*Lepida*	Pearly Parakeet
Psittacidae	*Pfrimeri*	Pfrimer's Parakeet
Psittacidae	*Picta*	Painted Parakeet
Psittacidae	*Rupicola*	Black-capped Parakeet
Cotingidae	*Purpurata*	Purple-throated Fruitcrow
Icteridae	*Lugubris*	Carib Grackle
Rallidae	*Longirostris*	Clapper Rail
Ramphastidae	*Dicolorus*	Red-breasted Toucan
Ramphastidae	*Toco*	Toco Toucan
Ramphastidae	*Tucanus*	White-throated Toucan
Ramphastidae	*Vitellinus*	Channel-billed Toucan
Polioptilidae	*Melanurus*	Long-billed Gnatwren
Thraupidae	*Bresilius*	Brazilian Tanager
Thraupidae	*Carbo*	Silver-beaked Tanager
Thraupidae	*Nigrogularis*	Masked Crimson Tanager
Trochilidae	*Naevius*	Saw-billed Hermit
Tyrannidae	*Fuscicauda*	Dusky-tailed Flatbill
Tyrannidae	*Megacephalum*	Large-headed Flatbill
Tyrannidae	*Ruficauda*	Rufous-tailed Flatbill
Rheidae	*Americana*	Greater Rhea, Common Rhea
Tyrannidae	*Olivaceus*	Olivaceous Flatbill
Tinamidae	*Rufescens*	Red-winged Tinamou

Family	Species	Common names (Eng)
Tyrannidae	*Immunda*	Pale-bellied Mourner
Tyrannidae	*Simplex*	Greyish Mourner
Hirundinidae	*Riparia*	Sand Martin
Podicipedidae	*Rolland*	White-tufted Grebe
Furnariidae	*Adusta*	Roraiman Barbtail
Rostratulidae	*Semicollaris*	South American Painted-snipe
Accipitridae	*Sociabilis*	Snail Kite
Cotingidae	*Rupicola*	Guianan Cock-of-the-rock
Laridae	*Niger*	Black Skimmer
Thamnophilidae	*Canadensis*	Black-crested Antshrike
Thamnophilidae	*Cristatus*	Silvery-cheeked Antshrike
Thamnophilidae	*Luctuosus*	Glossy Antshrike
Thamnophilidae	*Melanothorax*	Band-tailed Antshrike
Cardinalidae	*Atricollis*	Black-throated Saltator
Cardinalidae	*Aurantiirostris*	Golden-billed Saltator
Cardinalidae	*Coerulescens*	Greyish Saltator
Cardinalidae	*Fuliginosus*	Black-throated Grosbeak
Cardinalidae	*Grossus*	Slate-coloured Grosbeak
Cardinalidae	*Maxillosus*	Thick-billed Saltator
Cardinalidae	*Maximus*	Buff-throated Saltator
Cardinalidae	*Similis*	Green-winged Saltator
Cathartidae	*Papa*	King Vulture
Anatidae	*Melanotos*	Comb Duck
Tyrannidae	*Icterophrys*	Yellow-browed Tyrant
Cotingidae	*Major*	Greater Schiffornis
Cotingidae	*Turdina*	Thrush-like Schiffornis
Cotingidae	*Virescens*	Greenish Schiffornis
Thraupidae	*Melanopis*	Black-faced Tanager
Thraupidae	*Ruficapillus*	Cinnamon Tanager
Thamnophilidae	*Caurensis*	Caura Antbird
Thamnophilidae	*Leucostigma*	Spot-winged Antbird
Thamnophilidae	*Schistacea*	Slate-coloured Antbird
Furnariidae	*Phryganophilus*	Chotoy Spinetail
Thamnophilidae	*Naevia*	Silvered Antbird
Furnariidae	*Albigularis*	Grey-throated Leaftosser
Furnariidae	*Caudacutus*	Black-tailed Leaftosser
Furnariidae	*Mexicanus*	Tawny-throated Leaftosser
Furnariidae	*Rufigularis*	Short-billed Leaftosser
Furnariidae	*Scansor*	Rufous-breasted Leaftosser
Rhinocryptidae	*Iraiensis*	Marsh Tapaculo

Kingdom: Animalia

Family	Species	Common names (Eng)
Rhinocryptidae	Novacapitalis	Brasilia Tapaculo
Rhinocryptidae	Pachecoi	Planalto Tapaculo
Rhinocryptidae	Speluncae	Mouse-coloured Tapaculo
Parulidae	Noveboracensis	Northern Waterthrush
Ramphastidae	Gouldii	Gould's Toucanet
Ramphastidae	Maculirostris	Spot-billed Toucanet
Ramphastidae	Nattereri	Tawny-tufted Toucanet
Ramphastidae	Piperivora	Guianan Toucanet
Ramphastidae	Reinwardtii	Golden-collared Toucanet
Tyrannidae	Hypoleuca	River Tyrannulet
Tyrannidae	Munda	White-bellied Tyrannulet
Tyrannidae	Nigricans	Sooty Tyrannulet
Tyrannidae	Subcristata	White-crested Tyrannulet
Parulidae	Ruticilla	American Redstart
Emberizidae	Citrina	Stripe-tailed Yellow-finch
Emberizidae	Columbiana	Orange-fronted Yellow-finch
Emberizidae	Flaveola	Saffron Finch
Emberizidae	Luteola	Grassland Yellow-finch
Furnariidae	Ucayalae	Peruvian Recurvebill
Tyrannidae	Sibilator	Sirystes
Dendrocolaptidae	Griseicapillus	Olivaceous Woodcreeper
Formicariidae	Borbae	Pale-faced Antbird
Furnariidae	Maluroides	Bay-capped Wren-spinetail
Spheniscidae	Magellanicus	Magellanic Penguin
Cardinalidae	Americana	Dickcissel
Accipitridae	Melanoleucus	Black-and-white Hawk-eagle
Accipitridae	Ornatus	Ornate Hawk-eagle
Accipitridae	Tyrannus	Black Hawk-eagle
Emberizidae	Albogularis	White-throated Seedeater
Emberizidae	Americana	Wing-barred Seedeater
Emberizidae	Ardesiaca	Dubois's Seedeater
Emberizidae	Bouvreuil	Capped Seedeater
Emberizidae	Bouvronides	Lesson's Seedeater
Emberizidae	Caerulescens	Double-collared Seedeater
Emberizidae	Castaneiventris	Chestnut-bellied Seedeater
Emberizidae	Cinnamomea	Chestnut Seedeater
Emberizidae	Collaris	Rusty-collared Seedeater
Emberizidae	Falcirostris	Temminck's Seedeater
Emberizidae	Frontalis	Buffy-fronted Seedeater
Emberizidae	Hypochroma	Rufous-rumped Seedeater

LIST OF SPECIES

Family	Species	Common names (Eng)
Emberizidae	*Hypoxantha*	Tawny-bellied Seedeater
Emberizidae	*Intermedia*	Grey Seedeater
Emberizidae	*Melanops*	Hooded Seedeater
Emberizidae	*Minuta*	Ruddy-breasted Seedeater
Emberizidae	*Murallae*	Caqueta Seedeater
Emberizidae	*Nigricollis*	Yellow-bellied Seedeater
Emberizidae	*Nigrorufa*	Black-and-tawny Seedeater
Emberizidae	*Palustris*	Marsh Seedeater
Emberizidae	*Plumbea*	Plumbeous Seedeater
Emberizidae	*Ruficollis*	Dark-throated Seedeater
Emberizidae	*Schistacea*	Slate-coloured Seedeater
Steatornithidae	*Caripensis*	Oilbird
Scolopacidae	*Tricolor*	Wilson's Phalarope
Hirundinidae	*Ruficollis*	Southern Rough-winged Swallow
Thraupidae	*Diadematus*	Diademed Tanager
Trochilidae	*Lalandi*	Plovercrest
Laridae	*Antillarum*	Least Tern
Laridae	*Dougallii*	Roseate Tern
Laridae	*Forsteri*	Forster's Tern
Laridae	*Fuscata*	Sooty Tern
Laridae	*Hirundinacea*	South American Tern
Laridae	*Hirundo*	Common Tern
Laridae	*Maxima*	Royal Tern
Laridae	*Nilotica*	Gull-billed Tern
Laridae	*Paradisaea*	Arctic Tern
Laridae	*Sandvicensis*	Sandwich Tern
Laridae	*Superciliaris*	Yellow-billed Tern
Apodidae	*Biscutata*	Biscutate Swift
Apodidae	*Phelpsi*	Tepui Swift
Apodidae	*Zonaris*	White-collared Swift
Strigidae	*Huhula*	Black-banded Owl
Strigidae	*Hylophila*	Rusty-barred Owl
Strigidae	*Virgata*	Mottled Owl
Icteridae	*Defilippii*	Pampas Meadowlark
Icteridae	*Magna*	Eastern Meadowlark
Icteridae	*Militaris*	Red-breasted Blackbird
Icteridae	*Superciliaris*	White-browed Blackbird
Thamnophilidae	*Acutirostris*	Parana Antwren
Tyrannidae	*Islerorum*	Chapada Flycatcher, Chapada Suiriri
Tyrannidae	*Suiriri*	Suiriri Flycatcher, Chaco Suiriri

Family	Species	Common names (Eng)
Sulidae	*Dactylatra*	Masked Booby
Sulidae	*Leucogaster*	Brown Booby
Sulidae	*Sula*	Red-footed Booby
Furnariidae	*Albescens*	Pale-breasted Spinetail
Furnariidae	*Albigularis*	Dark-breasted Spinetail
Furnariidae	*Albilora*	White-lored Spinetail
Furnariidae	*Cabanisi*	Cabanis's Spinetail
Furnariidae	*Cherriei*	Chestnut-throated Spinetail
Furnariidae	*Cinerascens*	Grey-bellied Spinetail
Furnariidae	*Frontalis*	Sooty-fronted Spinetail
Furnariidae	*Gujanensis*	Plain-crowned Spinetail
Furnariidae	*Hypospodia*	Cinereous-breasted Spinetail
Furnariidae	*Infuscata*	Pinto's Spinetail
Furnariidae	*Kollari*	Hoary-throated Spinetail
Furnariidae	*Macconnelli*	Macconnell's Spinetail
Furnariidae	*Propinqua*	White-bellied Spinetail
Furnariidae	*Ruficapilla*	Rufous-capped Spinetail
Furnariidae	*Rutilans*	Ruddy Spinetail
Furnariidae	*Scutata*	Ochre-cheeked Spinetail
Furnariidae	*Spixi*	Spix's Spinetail
Furnariidae	*Whitneyi*	Bahia Spinetail
Furnariidae	*Dimidiata*	Russet-mantled Foliage-gleaner
Furnariidae	*Rufosuperciliata*	Buff-browed Foliage-gleaner
Ardeidae	*Sibilatrix*	Whistling Heron
Apodidae	*Squamata*	Fork-tailed Palm-swift
Podicipedidae	*Dominicus*	Least Grebe
Hirundinidae	*Albiventer*	White-winged Swallow
Hirundinidae	*Leucorrhoa*	White-rumped Swallow
Hirundinidae	*Meyeni*	Chilean Swallow
Thraupidae	*Coronatus*	Ruby-crowned Tanager
Thraupidae	*Cristatus*	Flame-crested Tanager
Thraupidae	*Luctuosus*	White-shouldered Tanager
Thraupidae	*Phoenicius*	Red-shouldered Tanager
Thraupidae	*Rufiventer*	Yellow-crested Tanager
Thraupidae	*Rufus*	White-lined Tanager
Thraupidae	*Surinamus*	Fulvous-crested Tanager
Tyrannidae	*Andrei*	Black-chested Tyrant
Thraupidae	*Callophrys*	Opal-crowned Tanager
Thraupidae	*Cayana*	Burnished-buff Tanager
Thraupidae	*Chilensis*	Paradise Tanager

Family	Species	Common names (Eng)
Thraupidae	*Cyanicollis*	Blue-necked Tanager
Thraupidae	*Cyanocephala*	Red-necked Tanager
Thraupidae	*Cyanoptera*	Black-headed Tanager
Thraupidae	*Cyanoventris*	Gilt-edged Tanager
Thraupidae	*Punctata*	Spotted Tanager
Thraupidae	*Schrankii*	Green-and-gold Tanager
Thraupidae	*Seledon*	Green-headed Tanager
Thraupidae	*Varia*	Dotted Tanager
Thraupidae	*Velia*	Opal-rumped Tanager
Thraupidae	*Xanthogastra*	Yellow-bellied Tanager
Tinamidae	*Nanus*	Dwarf Tinamou
Cuculidae	*Naevia*	Striped Cuckoo
Trochilidae	*Hypostictus*	Many-spotted Hummingbird
Thamnophilidae	*Major*	Great Antshrike
Tyrannidae	*Erythrurus*	Ruddy-tailed Flycatcher
Thraupidae	*Viridis*	Swallow Tanager
Thamnophilidae	*Divisorius*	Acre Antshrike
Thamnophilidae	*Doliatus*	Barred Antshrike
Thamnophilidae	*Insignis*	Streak-backed Antshrike
Thamnophilidae	*Murinus*	Mouse-coloured Antshrike
Thamnophilidae	*Nigrocinereus*	Blackish-grey Antshrike
Thamnophilidae	*Palliatus*	Chestnut-backed Antshrike
Thamnophilidae	*Pelzelni*	Planalto Slaty-antshrike
Thamnophilidae	*Punctatus*	Northern Slaty-antshrike
Thamnophilidae	*Ruficapillus*	Rufous-capped Antshrike
Thamnophilidae	*Schistaceus*	Plain-winged Antshrike
Thamnophilidae	*Stictocephalus*	Natterer's Slaty-antshrike
Threskiornithidae	*Caerulescens*	Plumbeous Ibis
Threskiornithidae	*Caudatus*	Buff-necked Ibis
Thraupidae	*Sordida*	Orange-headed Tanager
Thraupidae	*Bonariensis*	Blue-and-yellow Tanager
Thraupidae	*Cyanoptera*	Azure-shouldered Tanager
Thraupidae	*Palmarum*	Palm Tanager
Thraupidae	*Sayaca*	Sayaca Tanager
Trochilidae	*Leucurus*	Pale-tailed Barbthroat
Trochilidae	*Niger*	Sooty Barbthroat
Furnariidae	*Fusciceps*	Plain Softtail
Furnariidae	*Macroura*	Striated Softtail
Troglodytidae	*Coraya*	Coraya Wren
Troglodytidae	*Genibarbis*	Moustached Wren

Family	Species	Common names (Eng)
Troglodytidae	*Griseus*	Grey Wren
Troglodytidae	*Guarayanus*	Fawn-breasted Wren
Troglodytidae	*Leucotis*	Buff-breasted Wren
Troglodytidae	*Longirostris*	Long-billed Wren
Emberizidae	*Fuliginosus*	Sooty Grassquit
Emberizidae	*Obscurus*	Dull-coloured Grassquit
Ardeidae	*Fasciatum*	Fasciated Tiger-heron
Ardeidae	*Lineatum*	Rufescent Tiger-heron
Cotingidae	*Atra*	Black-and-gold Cotinga
Cotingidae	*Condita*	Grey-winged Cotinga
Tinamidae	*Guttatus*	White-throated Tinamou
Tinamidae	*Major*	Great Tinamou
Tinamidae	*Solitarius*	Solitary Tinamou
Tinamidae	*Tao*	Grey Tinamou
Cotingidae	*Cayana*	Black-tailed Tityra
Cotingidae	*Inquisitor*	Black-crowned Tityra
Cotingidae	*Semifasciata*	Masked Tityra
Tyrannidae	*Chrysocrotaphum*	Yellow-browed Tody-flycatcher
Tyrannidae	*Cinereum*	Common Tody-flycatcher
Tyrannidae	*Maculatum*	Spotted Tody-flycatcher
Tyrannidae	*Pictum*	Painted Tody-flycatcher
Tyrannidae	*Poliocephalum*	Yellow-lored Tody-flycatcher
Tyrannidae	*Assimilis*	Yellow-margined Flycatcher
Tyrannidae	*Flaviventris*	Yellow-breasted Flycatcher
Tyrannidae	*Poliocephalus*	Grey-crowned Flycatcher
Tyrannidae	*Sulphurescens*	Yellow-olive Flycatcher
Trochilidae	*Pella*	Crimson Topaz
Trochilidae	*Pyra*	Fiery Topaz
Psittacidae	*Huetii*	Scarlet-shouldered Parrotlet
Psittacidae	*Melanonotus*	Brown-backed Parrotlet
Psittacidae	*Purpuratus*	Sapphire-rumped Parrotlet
Psittacidae	*Surdus*	Golden-tailed Parrotlet
Thraupidae	*Melanops*	Black-goggled Tanager
Psittacidae	*Malachitacea*	Blue-bellied Parrot
Scolopacidae	*Flavipes*	Lesser Yellowlegs
Scolopacidae	*Melanoleuca*	Greater Yellowlegs
Scolopacidae	*Solitaria*	Solitary Sandpiper
Troglodytidae	*Aedon*	House Wren
Troglodytidae	*Rufulus*	Tepui Wren
Trogonidae	*Collaris*	Collared Trogon

LIST OF SPECIES

Family	Species	Common names (Eng)
Trogonidae	*Curucui*	Blue-crowned Trogon
Trogonidae	*Melanurus*	Black-tailed Trogon
Trogonidae	*Personatus*	Masked Trogon
Trogonidae	*Rufus*	Black-throated Trogon
Trogonidae	*Surrucura*	Surucua Trogon
Trogonidae	*Violaceus*	Violaceous Trogon
Trogonidae	*Viridis*	Amazonian White-tailed Trogon
Scolopacidae	*Subruficollis*	Buff-breasted Sandpiper
Turdidae	*Albicollis*	White-necked Thrush
Turdidae	*Amaurochalinus*	Creamy-bellied Thrush
Turdidae	*Flavipes*	Yellow-legged Thrush
Turdidae	*Fumigatus*	Cocoa Thrush
Turdidae	*Hauxwelli*	Hauxwell's Thrush
Turdidae	*Ignobilis*	Black-billed Thrush
Turdidae	*Lawrencii*	Lawrence's Thrush
Turdidae	*Olivater*	Black-hooded Thrush
Turdidae	*Rufiventris*	Rufous-bellied Thrush
Pipridae	*Stolzmanni*	Dwarf Tyrant-manakin
Pipridae	*Virescens*	Tiny Tyrant-manakin
Tyrannidae	*Sulphurea*	Sulphury Flycatcher
Tyrannidae	*Elatus*	Yellow-crowned Tyrannulet
Tyrannidae	*Albogularis*	White-throated Kingbird
Tyrannidae	*Dominicensis*	Grey Kingbird
Tyrannidae	*Melancholicus*	Tropical Kingbird
Tyrannidae	*Savana*	Fork-tailed Flycatcher
Tyrannidae	*Tyrannus*	Eastern Kingbird
Tytonidae	*Alba*	Barn Owl
Charadriidae	*Cayanus*	Pied Lapwing
Charadriidae	*Chilensis*	Southern Lapwing
Picidae	*Affinis*	Red-stained Woodpecker
Picidae	*Cassini*	Golden-collared Woodpecker
Picidae	*Kirkii*	Red-rumped Woodpecker
Picidae	*Maculifrons*	Yellow-eared Woodpecker
Vireonidae	*Altiloquus*	Black-whiskered Vireo
Vireonidae	*Flavoviridis*	Yellow-green Vireo
Vireonidae	*Gracilirostris*	Noronha Vireo
Vireonidae	*Olivaceus*	Red-eyed Vireo
Vireonidae	*Leucotis*	Slaty-capped Shrike-vireo
Emberizidae	*Jacarina*	Blue-black Grassquit
Thamnophilidae	*Poecilinotus*	Scale-backed Antbird

Family	Species	Common names (Eng)
Icteridae	*Flavus*	Saffron-cowled Blackbird
Pipridae	*Atronitens*	Black Manakin
Pipridae	*Uniformis*	Olive Manakin
Furnariidae	*Milleri*	Rufous-tailed Xenops
Furnariidae	*Minutus*	Plain Xenops
Furnariidae	*Rutilans*	Streaked Xenops
Furnariidae	*Tenuirostris*	Slender-billed Xenops
Cotingidae	*Albinucha*	White-naped Xenopsaris
Dendrocolaptidae	*Albicollis*	White-throated Woodcreeper
Dendrocolaptidae	*Falcirostris*	Moustached Woodcreeper
Dendrocolaptidae	*Major*	Great Rufous Woodcreeper
Cotingidae	*Atropurpurea*	White-winged Cotinga
Cotingidae	*Lamellipennis*	White-tailed Cotinga
Cotingidae	*Punicea*	Pompadour Cotinga
Dendrocolaptidae	*Elegans*	Elegant Woodcreeper
Dendrocolaptidae	*Fuscus*	Lesser Woodcreeper
Dendrocolaptidae	*Guttatus*	Buff-throated Woodcreeper
Dendrocolaptidae	*Obsoletus*	Striped Woodcreeper
Dendrocolaptidae	*Ocellatus*	Ocellated Woodcreeper
Tyrannidae	*Cinereus*	Grey Monjita
Tyrannidae	*Coronatus*	Black-crowned Monjita
Tyrannidae	*Dominicanus*	Black-and-white Monjita
Tyrannidae	*Irupero*	White Monjita
Tyrannidae	*Velatus*	White-rumped Monjita
Ardeidae	*Undulatus*	Zigzag Heron
Columbidae	*Auriculata*	Eared Dove
Emberizidae	*Capensis*	Rufous-collared Sparrow

Family	Species	Common names (Eng)
Gekkonidaex	*Gonatodes concinnatus*	Collared Streak Lizard
Gekkonidae	*Gonatodes hasemani*	Brown-Headed Streak Lizard
Gekkonidae	*Gonatodes humeralis*	Amazon Streak Lizard
Gekkonidae	*Lepidoblepharis festae,*	Brown Dwarf Gecko
Gekkonidae	*Lepidoblepharis (giant)*	Greater Dwarf Gecko
Gekkonidae	*Pseudogonatodes guianensis*	Amazon Pigmy Gecko
Gekkonidae	*Thecadactylus rapicaudus*	Turnip-Tailed Gecko
Hoplocercidae	*Enyalioides cofanorum,*	Cofan Wood Lizard
Hoplocercidae	*Enyalioides laticeps*	Amazon Wood Lizard
Hoplocercidae	*Enyalioides microlepis*	Brown Wood Lizard
Hoplocercidae	*Enyalioides palpebralis*	Horned Wood Lizard
Hoplocercidae	*Enyalioides praestabilis*	Blue-Spotted Wood Lizard
Iguanidae	*Iguana iguana*	Green Iguana
Polychrotidae	*Anolis bombiceps, fuscoauratus*	Blue-Lipped Anole
Polychrotidae	*Anolis fuscoauratus*	Slender Anole
Polychrotidae	*Anolis chrysolepis scypheus*	Yellow-Tongued Anole
Polychrotidae	*Anolis chrysolepis tandae*	Blue-Throated Anole
Polychrotidae	*Anolis punctatus*	Amazon Green Anole
Polychrotidae	*Anolis trachyderma*	Common Forest Anole
Polychrotidae	*Anolis transversalis*	Banded Tree Anole
Polychrotidae	*Anolis ortonii*	Bark Anole
Polychrotidae	*Polychrus liogaster,*	Southern Monkey Lizard
Polychrotidae	*Polychrus marmoratus*	Common Monkey Lizard
Tropiduridae	*Stenocercus fimbriatus,*	Western Leaf Lizard
Tropiduridae	*Stenocercus roseiventris*	Pink-Bellied Leaf Lizard
Tropiduridae	*Tropidurus (Uracentron) azureum guentheri*	Southern Green Thornytail
Tropiduridae	*Tropidurus (Uracentron) flaviceps*	Amazon Thornytail
Tropiduridae	*Tropidurus plica*	Collared Tree Lizard
Tropiduridae	*Tropidurus umbra ochrocollaris*	Blue-Lipped Tree Lizard
Gymnophthalmidae	*Alopoglossus atriventris,*	Keel-Bellied Shade Lizard
Gymnophthalmidae	*Alopoglossus angulatus,*	Large-Scaled Shade Lizard
Gymnophthalmidae	*Alopoglossus buckleyi,*	Smooth-Bellied Shade Lizard
Gymnophthalmidae	*Alopoglossus copii*	Drab Shade Lizard
Gymnophthalmidae	*Bachia trisanale trisanale*	Striped Worm Lizard
Gymnophthalmidae	*Bachia peruana*	Peruvian Worm Lizard
Gymnophthalmidae	*Bachia vermiformis*	Brown Worm Lizard
Gymnophthalmidae	*Leposoma parietale,*	Common Root Lizard
Gymnophthalmidae	*Leposoma percarinatum*	Striped Root Lizard
Gymnophthalmidae	*Leposoma snethlagei*	Brazilian Root Lizard

Family	Species	Common names (Eng)
Gymnophthalmidae	*Prionodactylus argulus,*	Elegant Eyed Lizard
Gymnophthalmidae	*Prionodactylus oshaugnessyi*	White-Striped Eyed Lizard
Teiidae	*Ameiva ameiva*	Amazon Racerunner
Teiidae	*Crocodilurus lacertinus*	Crocodile Tegu
Teiidae	*Dracaena guianensis*	Northern Caiman Lizard
Scincidae	*Mabuya bistriata*	Two-Lined Skink
Scincidae	*Mabuya nigropalmata*	Black-Handed Skink
Scincidae	*Mabuya nigropunctata*	Black-Spotted Skink
Leptotyphlopidae	*Leptotyphlops albifrons*	White-Fronted Threadsnake
Leptotyphlopidae	*Leptotyphlops diaplocius*	Amazonian Threadsnake
Leptotyphlopidae	*Leptotyphlops macrolepis*	Big-Eyed Threadsnake
Leptotyphlopidae	*Leptotyphlops signatus*	Peruvian Threadsnake
Typhlopidae	*Typhlops brongersmianus*	Black Blindsnake
Typhlopidae	*Typhlops minuisquamus*	White-Nosed Blindsnake
Typhlopidae	*Typhlops reticulatus*	Giant Blindsnake
Boidae	*Boa constrictor constrictor*	Red-Tailed Boa
Boidae	*Corallus caninus,*	Emerald Treeboa
Boidae	*Corallus hortulanus*	Amazon Treeboa
Boidae	*Epicrates cenchria*	Common Rainbow Boa
Boidae	*Eunectes murinus murinus*	Common Anaconda
Colubridae	*Atractus elaps*	ORNATE Earthsnake
Colubridae	*Atractus flammigerus*	Blotchedearthsnake
Colubridae	*Atractus latifrons*	Wedge-Tailed Earthsnake
Colubridae	*Atractus major*	Giant Earthsnake
Colubridae	*Chironius exoletus*	Common Whipsnake
Colubridae	*Chironius fuscus*	Olive Whipsnake
Colubridae	*Chironius multiventris multiventris,*	Long-Tailed Whipsnake
Colubridae	*Chironius scurrulus*	Rusty Whipsnake
Colubridae	*Dendrophidion dendrophis*	Common Forest Racers
Colubridae	*Dipsas catesbyi*	Ornate Thirst Snake
Colubridae	*Dipsas indica indica*	Big-Headed Thirst Snake
Colubridae	*Drepanoides anomalus*	Amazon Egg-Eater
Colubridae	*Erythrolamprus aesculapii aesculapii*	Common False Coralsnake
Colubridae	*Erythrolamprus guentheri*	Pink-Naped False Coralsnake
Colubridae	*Helicops leopardinus*	Spotted Watersnake
Colubridae	*Helicops pastazae*	Olive Watersnake
Colubridae	*Helicops polylepis*	Black-Chinned Watersnake
Colubridae	*Imantodes cenchoa,*	Blunt-Headed Treesnake
Colubridae	*Imantodes lentiferus*	Amazon Treesnake
Colubridae	*Leptophis ahaetulla nigromarginatus,*	Black-Skinned Parrot Snake

Family	Species	Common names (Eng)
Colubridae	*Leptophis cupreus*	Brown Parrot Snake
Colubridae	*Leptophis riveti*	Turquoise Parrot Snake
Colubridae	*Liophis breviceps breviceps*	Amazon Swampsnake
Colubridae	*Liophis cobellus dyticus*	South American Swampsnake
Colubridae	*Liophis oligolepis*	Stripe-Tailed Swampsnake
Colubridae	*Liophis reginae semilineatus*	Common Swampsnake
Colubridae	*Liophis miliaris chrysostomus*	White-Lipped Swampsnake
Colubridae	*Oxybelis aeneus*	Brown Vinesnake
Colubridae	*Oxybelis fulgidus*	Green Vinesnake
Colubridae	*Oxyrhopus m. melanogenys*	Black-Headed Calico Snake
Colubridae	*Oxyrhopus occipitalis*	Western Calico Snake
Colubridae	*Oxyrhopus petola digitalis*	Banded Calico Snake
Colubridae	*Pseudoboa coronata*	Amazon Scarletsnake
Colubridae	*Pseustes poecilonotus polylepis,*	Common Birdsnake
Colubridae	*Pseustes sulphureus sulphureus*	Giant Birdsnake
Colubridae	*Rhinobothryum lentiginosum*	Amazon Ringed Snake
Colubridae	*Siphlophis cervinus*	Common Liana Snake
Colubridae	*Spilotes pullatus pullatus*	Common Tiger Ratsnake
Colubridae	*Taeniophallus brevirostris*	Short-Nosed Groundsnake
Colubridae	*Taeniophallus occipitalis*	Spotted Groundsnake
Colubridae	*Tripanurgos compressus*	Red-Eyed Treesnake
Colubridae	*Umbrivaga pygmaea*	Pigmy Moss Snake
Colubridae	*Xenodon rabdocephalus rabdocephalus,*	Common False Viper
Colubridae	*Xenodon severus*	Giant False Viper
Viperidae	*Bothriopsis bilineata smaragdina,*	Western Striped Forest-Pitviper
Viperidae	*Bothriopsis taeniata taeniata*	Speckled Forest-Pitviper
Viperidae	*alcatraz*	Alcatrazes Lancehead
Viperidae	*insularis*	Golden Lancehead
Viperidae	*pirajai*	Piraja's Lancehead
Viperidae	*Lachesis muta muta*	Amazon Bushmaster
Elapidae	*Micrurus putumayensis*	Sooty Coralsnake
Elapidae	*Micrurus scutiventris*	Pigmy Black-Backed Coralsnake
Elapidae	*Micrurus spixii obscurus*	Amazonian Coralsnake
Elapidae	*Micrurus hemprichii ortonii*	Orange-Ringed Coralsnake
Elapidae	*Micrurus langsdorffi*	Langsdorff's Coralsnake
Elapidae	*Micrurus lemniscatus helleri*	South American Coralsnake
Elapidae	*Micrurus filiformis*	
Elapidae	*Micrurus narduccii narduccii*	Andean Black-Backed Coralsnake
Crocodylidae	*Paleosuchus palpebrosus,*	Dwarf Caiman

Family	Species	Common names (Eng)
Crocodylidae	*Paleosuchus trigonatus*	Smooth-Fronted Caiman
Crocodylidae	*Caiman crocodilus,*	Spectacled Caiman,
Crocodylidae	*Caiman niger*	Black Caiman
Testudinidae	*Geochelone carbonaria*	Redfoot Tortoise
	Geochelone denticulata	Yellowfoot Tortoise
Chelidae	*Platemys platycephala melanonota*	Western Twist-Necked Turtle
Chelidae	*Phrynops gibbus*	Lesser Toad-Headed Turtle
Chelidae	*Phrynops geoffroanus*	Spotted Toad-Headed Turtle
Chelidae	*Phrynops raniceps*	Greater Toad-Headed Turtle
Chelidae	*macrocephala*	Big-headed Pantanal Swamp Turtle
Chelidae	*radiolata*	Brazilian Radiolated Swamp Turtle
Chelidae	*rufipes*	Red-footed Sideneck Turtle
Chelidae	*Spixii*	Black Spine-necked Swamp Turtle
Chelidae	*Phrynops rufipes*	Red Toad-Headed Turtle
Pelomedusidae	*Peltocephalus dumerilianus*	Big-Headed River Turtle
Pelomedusidae	*Podocnemis expansa*	South American River Turtle
Pelomedusidae	*Podocnemis sextuberculata*	Amazon River Turtle,
Pelomedusidae	*Podocnemis unifilis*	Yellow-Spotted River Turtle

Family	Species	Common names (Eng)
Eleutherodactylidae	*Gutturosa*	Guiana Shield Frog
Dendrobatidae	*Flavopicta*	Lutz's Poison Frog
Dendrobatidae	*Picta*	Spot-legged Poison Frog
Hylidae	*Bokermanni*	Bokermann's Casque-headed Frog
Hylidae	*Brunoi*	Bruno's Casque-headed Frog
Brachycephalidae	*Didactylus*	Flea-frog
Brachycephalidae	*Ephippium*	Pumpkin Toadlet
Brachycephalidae	*Hermogenesi*	Flea-frog
Ceratophryidae	*Aurita*	Brazilian Horned Frog
Ceratophryidae	*Cornuta*	Amazonian Horned Frog
Ceratophryidae	*Cranwelli*	Chacoan Horned Frog
Ceratophryidae	*Joazeirensis*	Caatinga Horned Frog
Ceratophryidae	*Ornata*	Ornate Horned Frog
Dendrobatidae	*Leucomelas*	Yellow-headed Poison Frog
Dendrobatidae	*Tinctorius*	Dyeing Poison Frog
Leptodactylidae	*Myersi*	Myers' Thin-toed Frog
Leptodactylidae	*Paraensis*	Pará Thin-toed Frog
Leptodactylidae	*Vastus*	Northeastern Pepper Frog
Leiuperidae	*Henselii*	Hensel's Dwarf Frog
Pipidae	*Arrabali*	Arrabal's Suriname Toad
Pipidae	*Carvalhoi*	Carvalho's Surinam Toad
Pipidae	*Pipa*	Suriname Toad
Leiuperidae	*Bibroni*	Four-eyed Frog
Leiuperidae	*Brachyops*	Colombian Four-eyed Frog
Leiuperidae	*Diplolister*	Peters' Four-eyed Frog
Bufonidae	*Margaritifera*	South American Common Toad
Bufonidae	*Marina*	Cane Toad
Bufonidae	*Schneideri*	Cururu Toad
Hylidae	*Curicica*	Lanceback Treefrog
Hylidae	*Atlas*	Bokermann's Casque-headed Treefrog
Hylidae	*Nigromaculatus*	Black-spotted Casque-headed Treefrog

Family	Species	Common names (Eng)
Serranidae	*Afer*	Mutton Hamlet
Loricariidae	*Dolichopterus*	Bluechin xenocara, Bushymouth catfish
Haemulidae	*Moricandi*	Brownstriped Grunt
Osteoglossidae	*Gigas*	Arapaima, Pirarucu
Rivulidae	*Affinis*	Killifish
Balistidae	*Vetula*	Queen Triggerfish
Pimelodidae	*Rousseauxii*	Gilded catfish
Aspredinidae	*Coracoideus*	Catfish
Aspredinidae	*Knerii*	Banjo catfish
Rivulidae	*Brucei*	Santa Catarina Sabrefin
Serranidae	*Fulva*	Lemon-yellow Butterfish
Lebiasinidae	*Nigrofasciata*	Blackband Copella
Callichthyidae	*Adolfoi*	Adolf's catfish
Callichthyidae	*Melini*	Bandit corydoras
Cichlidae	*Lepidota*	Pike cichlid
Rivulidae	*Boitonei*	Brasilia Lyrefin
Rivulidae	*Constanciae*	Annual Tropical Killifish
Curimatidae	*Voga*	Characin
Serranidae	*Inermis*	Donkey Fish
Characidae	*Terofali*	Tetra
Gymnotidae	*Electricus*	Electric eel
Serranidae	*Adscensionis*	Rock Hind
Serranidae	*Flavolimbatus*	Yellowedge Grouper
Serranidae	*Itajara*	Goliath Grouper
Serranidae	*Marginatus*	Dusky Grouper
Serranidae	*Morio*	Red Grouper
Serranidae	*Nigritus*	Black Grouper
Serranidae	*Niveatus*	Seabass
Serranidae	*Hispanus*	Spanish Flag
Characidae	*Hyanuary*	Costello tetra
Syngnathidae	*Reidi*	Longsnout Seahorse
Characidae	*Bentosi*	Ornate Tetra
Characidae	*Megalopterus*	Black phantom tetra
Characidae	*Pulchripinnis*	Lemon tetra
Pristigasteridae	*Amazonica*	Amazon ilisha
Anostomidae	*Striatus*	Characin, Striped leporinus
Rivulidae	*Marmoratus*	Ginger Pearlfish
Rivulidae	*Minimus*	Minute Pearlfish
Rivulidae	*Opalescens*	Opalescent Pearlfish
Rivulidae	*Splendens*	Splendid Pearlfish

Family	Species	Common names (Eng)
Auchenipteridae	*Oncinus*	Jaguar catfish
Lutjanidae	*Analis*	Mutton Snapper
Lutjanidae	*Cyanopterus*	Canteen Snapper
Serranidae	*Acutirostris*	Comb Grouper
Serranidae	*Bonaci*	Black Rockfish
Serranidae	*Interstitialis*	Grey Mannock
Serranidae	*Microlepis*	Charcoal Belly
Serranidae	*Tigris*	Tiger Grouper
Serranidae	*Venenosa*	Yellowfin Grouper
Osteoglossidae	*Ferreirai*	Black arawana, Black aruana
Sparidae	*Pagrus*	Red Porgy
Serranidae	*Furcifer*	Creole-fish
Polyprionidae	*Americanus*	Wreckfish
Chaetodontidae	*Obliquus*	Oblique Butterflyfish
Loricariidae	*Lima*	Catfish
Scaridae	*Guacamaia*	Rainbow Parrotfish
Prochilodontidae	*Taeniurus*	Silver prochilodus
Loricariidae	*Evansii*	Catfish
Hypopomidae	*Elegans*	Barred Knifefish
Cichlidae	*Centisquama*	Slender pike cichlid
Scombridae	*Alalunga*	Albacore Tuna
Scombridae	*Albacares*	Yellowfin Tuna
Scombridae	*Maccoyii*	Southern Bluefin Tuna
Scombridae	*Obesus*	Bigeye Tuna
Scombridae	*Thynnus*	Northern Bluefin Tuna
Xiphiidae	*Gladius*	Swordfish